GLOBAL VILLAGE IDIOT

Global Village Idiot

Dubya, Dumb Jokes, and
One Last Word Before You Vote

John O'Farrell

Grove Press
New York

Originally published in 2001 by Doubleday in Great Britain in a slightly different form.

Published simultaneously in Canada
Printed in the United States of America

FIRST AMERICAN EDITION

Library of Congress Cataloging-in-Publication Data

O'Farrell, John.
    Global village idiot / John O'Farrell.
       p. cm.
    ISBN 0-8021-4038-6
    1. Great Britain—Social life and customs—1945–   2. Great Britain—Politics and government—1997–   3. United States—Politics and government—2001–
I. Title.

DA589.4.O38 2003
941.085'9—dc21   2003049207

Grove Press
841 Broadway
New York, NY 10003
04 05 06 07 08   10 9 8 7 6 5 4 3 2 1

Contents

GLOBAL VILLAGE IDIOT

INTRODUCTION

My mother grew up during World War II and doesn't like to waste anything. So when she had a new hip joint fitted recently she asked the doctor if she could take the old bone home for her dog. I suppose I should just be grateful that she didn't boil it up to make a delicious stock. "What sort of soup is this, Mother?" "It's Mom's hipbone and country vegetable." I told my friends this story and we all had a good chuckle. But then I overheard one of them telling someone else and as more laughter echoed around the pub I thought, "Hang on, what gives you the right to laugh at my family?" And so it is with poking fun at your own country and its government. It's all very well for Americans to satirize the Bush administration, but that doesn't give every liberal limey the right to start sniping at the U.S. president.

Thus it is with some trepidation and a sense of humility that I offer this collection of essays to you from the other side of the Atlantic. I love the United States and its people whom I know have a great sense of humour, so please do not think that any criticism of your president or Republican Party policies is an attack on you as a patriotic American (unless you yourself happen to be reading this, Dubya, which—let's face it—is unlikely given the absence of pictures). It is because the United States has historically been a beacon of free expression and democracy that I worry about the direction in which its government is now leading the free world. You did a great job throwing off the hereditary monarchy of George III. It just seems strange that you adopted the hereditary presidency of George II.

I also have great respect for the American traditions of free speech as enshrined in the First Amendment, and I was sort of hoping that this right might extend to non-U.S. citizens who aspire to noble American values (i.e., making a quick buck by selling a load of jokes that have been printed in British newspapers once already). My country is said to have a special relationship with America, which is very important to us here in Britain, if only as an excellent way to annoy the French. So I hope you understand that any jokes at your country's expense from this particular Brit are very much in the spirit of a critical friend. Okay, maybe one of those friends who stole your girlfriend and still owes you money and never calls you except to ask unreasonable favours, but a friend nonetheless. With a degree of distance from the United States and the American media it could even be that a British eye on topical events might offer a fresh perspective. Some things seem normal just because things have always been that way where we happen to live. When Vlad the Impaler was prince of Wallachia, many of his subjects were shocked at the radical suggestions of visitors from abroad. "What, stop impaling people altogether?!! Surely you mean gradually introduce some form of licensed impaling after hearing evidence from the Guild of Impalers?"

In fact most of these pieces are not about American politics at all. Instead I have sought to cover as wide a range of topics as possible, from human cloning to the Miss World competition to soft-core pornography. (Come to think of it, these are all the same subject, aren't they?) I have tried to avoid banging on and on about the issues that really bug me because I thought it might get a bit boring for people to keep reading about car alarms and the uncooperative nature of my printer. Most of the essays are about three pages each—the idea being that you can sit down and read one piece a day, or possibly two, depending on whether you had All-Bran or boiled eggs for breakfast. Or perhaps you are travelling and keep being interrupted by a fellow passenger chatting to you, or maybe you're distracted by those bits of molten engine casing dropping off the wing, and in these situations it can be hard to concentrate on some major literary classic. But like the novels of Jackie Collins you can read this book in any random order and it will make no difference whatsoever to how much you enjoy it.

This collection begins with George W. Bush well on the way to getting his new job, and ends soon after Saddam Hussein loses his. Where there is some topical or peculiarly British reference that might need further clarification I've inserted an asterisk to denote that there will be an explanatory footnote at the bottom of the page.* I have left in the dates that the pieces first appeared although most of them are about issues that are very much still with us. This is only one person's reaction to the great events and profound moral issues that are shaping the new ~~milennium millenium~~ century. But as America heads toward the next presidential election I hope there may be a few things here worth remembering before you vote. Most importantly I hope this collection raises the occasional smile in a time when there seems to be less and less to laugh about. As the old saying goes, "You either laugh or you cry." Or you think of Dubya being elected to a second term and you do both.

JO'F—London, 2003

*Yup, you've got the hang of that pretty quickly.

P.S. My apologies are offered for any factual inaccuracies discovered subsequent to publication, but all details have been thoroughly researched by spending five minutes on the Internet and then giving up. For example, to check the story of nurses giving sex education in schools, I called up the search engine and entered the words "nurses" and "sex." And then I was thrown out of my local library.

GLOSSARY

Scientists have discovered that not only do dolphins have their own language, but they even have a fully developed sense of humour with complex riddles and jokes. Zoologists have just spent months decoding the following dolphin gag: "Why did the pilot whale swim inshore? Because the tide was going out!" Okay, I know, I know. It loses something in translation. It's often not much better when comedy travels from one country to another (although it can work the other way; I co-wrote a sitcom that bombed on the BBC and was a huge hit in Belgium. Boy, was that a great comfort!).

These essays were originally written for publication in Britain and so there may be times in this collection where certain words or expressions might confuse the American reader, phrases like "world powers such as Britain" or "Tony Blair has persuaded George Bush." Perhaps I should also quickly explain a little bit about Britain's political parties. Much like the United States, Britain has a two-party system to ensure that the voters are guaranteed a genuine choice of rather similar policies. Tony Blair's Labour Party has been more radical and left-wing in the past, but annoyingly this tended to coincide with the periods when it didn't get elected. The Conservative Party is more right-wing; indeed it is currently disappearing so far off the scale that Darth Vader has just cancelled his membership. But the big difference that you have to understand about Britain is that it all comes down to social class. Britain has never really recovered from the Battle of Hastings in 1066, when the French came over and rather rudely installed themselves as the despotic rulers of all England. And to this day the Conservative upper classes still drink wine and have cottages in France, whereas the Saxon serfs still drink beer and use unprintable Anglo-Saxon vocabulary. The Labour Party was established to be Robin Hood, to steal from the rich and give to the poor, although somewhere along the way Robin seems to have got himself a nice big castle and pulled up the drawbridge. That is one concept I imagine does not need translating.

George Bernard Shaw famously said that Britain and the United States were two nations separated by a common language. There are many examples where words have very different meanings on either side of the Atlantic, and below are listed a few more examples that will hopefully help to prevent any misunderstandings. In Britain the most common slang word for cigarette is "fag." On one live U.S. chat show a British comedian drew shocked gasps from the audience when he said that he was never happy unless he had a fag in his mouth. Mind you, it made for an interesting after-show party. . . .

American	English
Sidewalk	Pavement
Faucet	Tap
Trash	American daytime television
American foreign policy	Allied policy
Movie with British second assistant director	Anglo-American production
The World Series	Local championship for minority sport
Soccer World Cup (minority sport favoured by girls and Hispanics)	World Cup (most important sporting, cultural, and political event in the entire universe, especially in 1966 when England won it)
Hooray! My team won!	Oh dear. My team won but played rather badly.
All-day breakfast	All-day breakfast (not available after 11 A.M.)
Waiter, this food sucks!	Shh, dear, best not make a fuss.

NOT SUCH A "SUPER TUESDAY" IF DUBYA WINS IT . . .

7 March 2000

The first Europeans to reach the Pacific coast of North America observed a bizarre custom practiced by the Kwakiutl natives in which tribal leaders would challenge each other to what was called a "potlatch." This involved the two chiefs going to the cliff's edge and throwing items of immense value into the sea to demonstrate their village's enormous wealth. Blankets, copper pots, weapons; they took turns to chuck away everything that they needed to survive as their two tribes looked on and gasped at their leaders' courage. The first one who ran out of valuables was the loser. And the explorers watched all this and thought, "Great—that's how we'll choose our president!"

Today is Super Tuesday in the United States of America. The only accurate part of this description is that it is indeed a Tuesday. It's not really that "super" that a number of states hold primary elections on the same day. "Incredible Waste of Money Tuesday" might be a better name. Call me a sceptic, but it cannot be a good thing that the leader of the free world is chosen on the basis of who has the most balloons. The battle for nominations and the race to become president has now become a permanent cycle of massive fund-raising and profligate spending, and as Bush has demonstrated yet again, the candidate who accumulates the most dollars wins his party's nomination. Why can't they just be honest about it? Instead of spending months flying around the country accusing each other of being soft on crime or dithering on abortion, why doesn't Bush get his wallet out and say to McCain, "Okay, let's get this over with—how much have you got?" And they'd count out all the dollars they've been given and whoever has the most enormous pile gets onto the Republican ticket. Then Bush could take the stand and shout "God Bless Money!" as everyone whooped, clapped, and held up banners saying "Whoever's richest for the White House!"

Al Gore seems to have already wrapped up the Democratic nomination on the basis that while Bill Clinton was president, he was right by his side. I only hope he averted his eyes on occasion. But he too has spent tens of millions of dollars and will spend as much again when the election proper gets under way. When Lincoln dedicated the cemetery at Gettysburg, his address was only slightly wrong: *These dead shall not have died in vain—that this nation under God shall have a new birth of freedom, and that government of the billionaires, by the billionaires, for the billionaires shall not perish from this earth.*

John McCain effectively lost his battle to become the Republican candidate last October when a bill he had cosponsored to limit spending in U.S. presidential elections was defeated in the senate. Amid accusations of dirty tricks, a filibuster to prevent proper debate on the bill was passed by just five votes and so the twentieth attempt in the last twelve years to reform financing of elections was thrown out. Yet again America's super-rich are free to throw money at the candidate they think least likely to take any serious money off them once they are in the White House. Meanwhile the majority of poor Americans who are offered nothing by either party take no part in the whole process and an apartheid of apathy is created.

It would be interesting to see the same system used to appoint the British head of state. The Queen's fortune would be used up in a couple of months buying television prime time to persuade us that the Windsors really were one big happy family and that her husband was not going to go all liberal on gun control. Once the cash had run out she would have to have fund-raising dinners with various show-biz millionaires, pretending to be amused when a celebrity soccer player put a whoopee cushion on her throne. In Britain we have far fewer elections but at least most British citizens actually take part in a general election, even if you can hear them making their choice in the polling booths by saying "Ippy-dippy-dation, my operation, how many people at the station . . ." But as ever, the trend is toward the American way. At the last British general election both major parties spent (or arguably threw away) millions of pounds without shifting their poll position one iota. There is an inevitable equation that states that the more money political parties require, the less democratic the political system will become.

It is because today's American presidential hopefuls are so beholden to their financial backers that there could never be a candidate with a real programme to tackle America's growing inequalities. The people who need representing the most will not be voting this supine Tuesday. And because of the narrowness of the remaining constituency, none of the candidates can suggest any vaguely sensible policies like introducing gun control, abolishing capital punishment, or calling a halt to any more *Police Academy* spin-offs. There is the additional problem that with so much power shifting to the hands of the multinationals, the election of national figureheads is looking increasingly irrelevant. Perhaps the real focus should be on the business leaders who really run the world. Imagine what the election rallies would be like for the chairman of the world's biggest companies: "My fellow shareholders—although we have done very well to win power from the politicians, this is no time for complacency. We must not rest until every rain forest is chopped down, every twelve-year-old in Africa smokes sixty cigarettes a day, and every street corner has an abandoned McDonald's chocolate shake leaking across the pavement." The delegates' hearts would be filled with pride at such lofty ambition. And our elected politicians could stand outside the conference center, waving their placards from behind the crash barrier, demanding to be listened to. Tony Blair would shout, "What do we want?" and Jacques Chirac would refuse to join in because he didn't shout in French. And the riot police would throw tear gas and Bill Clinton would show everyone how not to inhale.

It is because of the growing power of private companies compared to nation states that they are able to exert such influence over who wins the nominations for the American presidency. If George W. Bush emerges as the front-runner today, he will not be the Republican Party candidate so much as the Oil Company Candidate. His father is the ex-president, and the son will be the Exxon-president. It's worth looking at the background of the Republican front-runner, if only to marvel at how such a complex democracy of 250 million people can end up with the worst possible outcome since Henry Kissinger won the Nobel Peace Prize.

George W. likes to make out that he had a typical American background, no different than any other wholesome American family in which Dad was head of the CIA. No doubt when they were kids George and his brother could be heard playing in the backyard: "Come on Jeb, let's play destabilizing third world governments." After an expensive education that resulted in only mediocre grades, George Jr. took the traditional route for future American politicians and jumped the line for the National Guard to avoid going to Vietnam. One day they will make moving Vietnam films about all those future politicians that dodged the draft: *Staying*

Home; Full Tweed Jacket; Good Morning Houston; and *The Beer Hunter.*

In 1981 Dad became vice president, which seemed to coincide with the time that George Jr. found it easier to get backers for his oil company. Despite his connections his various oil businesses all foundered, and though his investors lost millions, George W. somehow always managed to emerge with his personal wealth increased. Who needs oil when Dad's there to oil the wheels for you?

Even more murky are his financial dealings with the Texas Rangers baseball team. Bush put together a consortium of millionaires to buy the club, and got himself made managing director even though he put up less than 1 percent of the money himself. A brand-new stadium was built with public money. This greatly increased the value of the club but of course none of this cash was returned to the taxpayer when it was sold again. George pocketed a cool $14.9 million and became the man who put the "base" into baseball.

The association with the Texas Rangers made him a local celebrity and, against expectations, he was elected governor. He worked very hard in Texas, signing more death warrants than all the other state governors put together, even executing juvenile offenders and senior citizens. We're used to politicians who'd be prepared to sell their own grandmothers, but now we've got one who would electrocute them as well. He broke a few other records, too: Texas now has the worst water pollution and air quality of any of the major states. Bush consistently took the side of big business against the interest of ordinary Texans and what he did for the Lone Star State, he now hopes to do for all fifty. It couldn't be better for the multinationals if Ronald McDonald himself had got the presidency. In fact Ronald probably would have got the Republican nomination if it wasn't so obvious that he wore makeup.

Super Tuesday looks like it will be followed by Suicidal Wednesday, as the world wakes up to the possibility that this man could make it all the way to the White House. Of course at this early stage in the American presidential campaign it would be foolish for me to attempt to predict that George W. Bush will actually be elected, especially if this article were ever to be reprinted in some collection or other. Were my political forecasts to be proved correct, people would only think I'd added this bit in after the event. Nevertheless I'm prepared to stick my neck out and guess that Dubya will not only win the Republican nomination but also the American presidency, although I think it will be a very close call. Maybe there will even be a controversy about confusing ballot papers and endless recounts in states such as, say, Florida; and then later President Bush will go to war against Iraq to finish what his father started; oh, and Brazil will beat Germany 2–0 in the World Cup final; and Miramax films will make a movie of the musical *Chicago*, which will win six Academy Awards including an Oscar for Catherine Zeta-Jones, as well as for best costumes, best editing, and cinematography. But then, you know, who can possibly guess what might really happen in the next few years?

THE END OF THE WORLD IS NIGH—APPOINT A TASK FORCE

9 March 2000

Sixty-five million years ago the dinosaurs were wiped out when a huge asteroid struck Earth. When you think about it, this was an incredibly bad bit of luck—that all the world's dinosaurs happened to be standing in the same place at the time. Maybe they were attending a conference on the dangers of asteroids. The triceratops that were being laughed at for insisting that there was a very real danger must have felt pretty smug in the last few seconds before they all copped it.

But now the problem is apparently back again. This week the British government appointed a task force to look into the dangers posed by meteorites. Research on this front has been slow to develop. No money was spent during the 1980s because President Reagan was confident that if an asteroid was going to destroy Earth, then Superman would fly up and punch it back into outer space. Now at last various countries are waking up to the danger. So who is Britain's real-life superhero who is going to save us from obliteration in the manner of Bruce Willis in *Armageddon*? Step forward Sir Crispin

Tickell, chancellor of Kent University and prominent environmentalist. Pah, what chance do the asteroids have now?!

The effects of falling meteorites do make for some frightening reading. A relatively small meteorite would destroy an area the size of Detroit. The problem is that there is no guarantee that it would indeed be Detroit. A larger rock, such as the six-mile-wide asteroid that hit the earth at the end of the Cretaceous era, would trigger a nuclear winter, acid rain, forest fires, and a series of devastating sea waves causing massive global floods. Still, as long as you've got your health, eh? But just imagine having to watch the astrologist on Breakfast TV giving us the predictions from his look at the stars: "You stubborn Leos are all going to be wiped out as well, I'm afraid . . . you may find yourself feeling edgy and nervous all morning and then very flat in the afternoon. . . ."

It's been claimed this week that individually we have a greater chance of being killed by a falling asteroid than we do of winning the lottery. I must confess that I have a problem with this statistic. Every Saturday night we learn that there is one lucky jackpot winner who lives in the West Midlands. They do not tell us ". . . and this week's unfortunate victim of a falling meteorite lived in the Great Yarmouth area. And remember, if no one is killed by falling space debris then it is a rollover week and the asteroid will be twice as big on Wednesday night!" In reality the chances of a huge meteorite hitting the earth are extremely remote and more importantly there is very little we could do if one did. You could try putting on your cycle helmet, I suppose, but against a rock several miles wide travelling at seventy thousand miles an hour this would probably offer limited protection. Scientists have been talking with great confidence how a nuclear missile could be fired at the incoming rock to deflect it off course but I am not convinced. If our smart bombs cannot even avoid the Chinese embassy in Belgrade then what chance does a one-off missile have of hitting a rock travelling at twenty miles a second? It's not as if we could go back to the suppliers after the earth had been destroyed and ask them for our money back.

For every issue of public safety there is a political equation that has to be applied. "How big is the risk?" divided by "Can we afford to do anything about it?" The grim truth is that there are some cosmic dangers that we tiny humans are powerless to do anything about. Eventually the earth will spin out of its orbit or the sun will burn out or some cataclysmic space event will occur that will end life on earth. It's a shame but at least it will give you the chance to tell Marjorie in Accounts that you love her. In the meantime there are millions of avoidable deaths that occur every year through unnecessary poverty, preventable diseases, or wars that should never be fought. These things are the real disasters, not the risk of some lumps of old comet falling out of space. What we have to do to save Planet Earth is bring these issues to the top of our political agenda and the world leaders will be forced to really step up and save the world. Ha! And we thought the chances of being struck by a meteorite were remote. . . .

FROM HERE TO PATERNITY

12 March 2000

This week new paternity rights became law: British parents are now entitled to thirteen weeks' leave after their children are born. Because the leave is unpaid there is a risk that only the very rich will be able to afford it, leaving the newborn baby with a Croatian teenage au pair while they have a month's skiing followed by two months in the Maldives. But clearly it is a big step in the right direction. Now men cannot be sacked for taking time off work to be with their newborn babies. "Damn!" they'll all be thinking, ". . . now I'll have to come up with another excuse."

The rights came into effect yesterday—with the bizarre consequence that parents of any baby born before midnight on Tuesday were not eligible. In labour wards up and down the land you could hear midwives shouting, "Don't push!" or "Okay, the baby's head is out. . . . Now could you just hang on like that for another forty-seven minutes?" In the case of twins born on either side of midnight I suppose the parents get the statutory thirteen weeks' leave, but to stay within the spirit of the law they should make an effort not to bond with the older one.

The legislation is part of the government's very laudable plan to get fathers more involved with the care of their newborn children. But the question that is on everyone's lips at Westminster is, Will the man who made this legislation possible take advantage of it himself? Of course Tony Blair will be there at the birth of his fourth child, encouraging his wife to "Meet the challenge of the new millennium." But then what? Will he just go back to work? Most men like to make out that their job is really important and, as Prime Minister Tony Blair does, possibly have a case. But he would be contradicting all the government's messages about parenting if he did not at least take some time off work.

What will make it harder for Tony Blair is that not only does he work at home, but even if he did try to take some time off, ministers would still keep coming round to his house, stepping over the buggy in the hallway to have meetings in the Cabinet Room. How is Tony supposed to just ignore that? With the baby in his arms he would put his ear to the door and hear all the old Labour socialist tendencies resurfacing without him. "So that's agreed then, we'll renationalize all the public utilities without compensation to shareholders . . ." and then Tony will tentatively put his head around the door.

"Oh hi, Tony!"

"Sorry, did I hear something about renationalization?"

"Oh don't worry about any of that. You carry on looking after the baby. See you in thirteen weeks . . ."

'Right, um—nothing I can help with?"

"Tony—I think that babygrow looks like it needs changing . . ."

The other alternative is for Tony to take the baby to work with him. Nothing could be more disarming than a party leader standing in the House of Commons with a little baby wriggling in his arms. The angry hostility of Prime Minister's Questions would evaporate overnight.

"Madam Speaker, is the Prime Minister aware that his new baby is really really lovely and looks just like his dad?"

"Madam Speaker—this may be the case, but I think if the honourable members opposite were to look at these photos of our babies that were born under the last Conservative government they will find that they looked much more like their mum."

That's what happens when there is a baby present. It completely takes over as the focus of attention in the room. A shadow minister might deliver the most damning speech on government policy, with shocking statistics, brilliant quotes, and a blistering personal attack on the prime minister. But while the baby is trying to grab Madam Speaker's little finger, no one is going to take the slightest bit of notice. With a bit of training it could probably even learn to be sick every time the leader of the opposition starts speaking.

Foreign heads of state will have to meet the prime minister when he is free, namely at half past three in the morning when it's Tony's turn to get up. The weekly audience with the Queen may lose some of its formality. "Can you just take that dirty nappy out to the dustbin please, Your Majesty, Baby's just gone and wee'd all over the changing mat."

Frankly it's very hard seeing the prime minister doing any of this. He can't just give up work, yet he cannot be seen not to set an example. There is only one foreseeable outcome. Although pregnancies are generally always forty weeks long, soon we can expect an announcement that the government cannot find the time for the birth of the baby during the next parliamentary session and that the baby cannot be delivered this side of the general election. It may seem a bit hard on Mrs. Blair but many of the homeless and the unemployed have had to learn to wait for Labour promises to be delivered. Cherie will just have to hold on as well. Women used to go into labour after nine months. "New labour" takes a little bit longer.

ECUMENICAL WITH THE TRUTH

14 March 2000

Most of us find the act of apologising an awkward and embarrassing experience, but being infallible for two thousand years can't make it any easier. On Sunday Pope John Paul II shocked his congregation by breaking with centuries of tradition and saying sorry. He apologised for the persecution of the Jews, he apologised for the oppression of women, he apologised for the use of violence and torture down the centuries, and he apologised for the time he reversed the Popemobile into another car and didn't leave a note.

Worshipers knew that something was up when the pontiff arrived at St. Peter's dressed in purple. The colour signifies penitence and contrition, so they thought either he's going to ask forgiveness for something or he's now got so old that he's completely lost any sort of dress sense. Of course it is possible that the whole thing was a spontaneous aberration, brought about by the stress of giving up the ciggies and booze for Lent. But his apologies on behalf of the Catholic church were widely welcomed. Apparently the Northern Ireland Protestants shrugged and said, "Hey, that's all right mate, don't worry about it . . ."

Now that the Vatican has sought forgiveness for the sins committed in its name, surely it is now time that the Church of England followed suit. The Archbishop of Canterbury must apologise at once for the misery caused by the Young Christians Good News Coffee Morning. He must seek absolution for the torture that was the Harvest Festival Bring and Buy Sale. He must apologise that we have all been embarrassed into self-consciously mouthing half-remembered hymns at weddings and christenings. I have no fear of Hell now that I've heard a group of thirty-something atheists mumbling their way through "I Know That My Redeemer Liveth."

There are of course some genuine atrocities that have been committed in the name of religion by the British since the Reformation, not least in Ireland, but the Vatican represents a much older and popular church and can therefore boast a far more impressive list of historical outrages. The pope was indirectly apologising for just about everything done in the name of the Christian religion since St. Peter first went round knocking on people's doors asking them if they had heard the good news about Jesus. It must have been a great comfort to those witches burnt at the stake to think that in four hundred years' time someone was going to say sorry for it all.

The way things seem to work in the Catholic church are that it doesn't matter how heinous your sins are, as long as you acknowledge them. On Sunday the pope effectively went into confession and asked for forgiveness for persecuting millions of people for countless centuries and the priest replied, "Oh well, my child, it was all a long time ago; say a couple of 'Hail Mary's and be on your way . . ."

This is a great scam that Catholics everywhere should now start trying themselves. "Forgive me, Father, for I have sinned. My great-great-grandfather on my mother's side took part in repressing the Indian Mutiny."

"Are you sure there is nothing else more recent you want to confess?"

"Well yes, there's my granny of course, she originally defended Stalin's persecution of the kulaks."

It's easy to apologise for atrocities that happened hundreds of years ago, such as the Crusades and the conquistadors and Charlton Heston's first NRA rally. The point is that there are terrible things happening today that the pope has the power to change. While the AIDS epidemic sweeps through Africa, the Vatican has decreed that the provision of condoms in the area would be a sin. An incalculable number of unnecessary deaths occurs every year because of this one tenet of outdated dogma. If the pope is trying to tell us that religion doctrine does not continue to cause suffering he is being ecumenical with the truth. Will we have to wait five hundred years before Pope Gladys V admits that this was wrong, or will today's Vatican look to their own sins rather than those of their forefathers?

Of course it is possible that by then there will be no organised Christian religion. Now that the Vatican has unpicked one of the central tenets of Catholicism, the whole edifice of the church could begin to crumble. In that sense Canterbury is centuries ahead of Rome, for the pope is acknowledging things we have taken for granted in the UK for years. And now the new national religion of Britain is agnosticism. Every Sunday morning millions of English worshippers head down to Home Depot. There they pray that the special offer on that hedge trimmer still gets them loyalty points on their reward card. On the Sabbath evening the family comes together and watches football, and on each holy day they will get in the Range Rover and make a pilgrimage to the Miracle Mile. Since we began to doubt the word of our own religious leaders, much of Western civilisation has turned into a nation of agnostic fundamentalists. It almost makes you nostalgic for the Spanish Inquisition.

DON'T BAN FOX HUNTING—
IT'S FAR TOO UNPOPULAR

18 March 2000

O pponents of fox hunting say that it belongs to another century but I for one am glad that fox hunters have failed to move with the times. The phenomenon of urban foxes has thankfully not given rise to urban fox hunting. It's bad enough having a wild fox in my back garden in London; I don't want a load of foxhounds and stallions leaping over from next door and galloping all over my begonias. But then what right do I have to object—we city folk just don't understand the ways of the country, do we?

What I still haven't figured out is, if fox hunting really is a sport, how come the same side always wins? Does this always come as a surprise to the participants? Do the hunters look on excitedly with their fingers crossed to see whether the fox rips the dogs to pieces or vice versa? You don't get the fox being interviewed on *Sports-night* beforehand saying, "Well Brian, I'm really confident about this one, I've had a couple of fights in the run-up; there was that easy win against Mr. Rabbit, but this is the big one I've been training for."

"So you're not worried that the bookies have you at 1000–1 against beating this pack of foxhounds?"

"What, you mean there's more than one of them? Er, excuse me—
I've just got to call my agent."

It appears that the pro-hunters were given a lifeline last year with
the announcement of an inquiry into the effects of a ban on rural
life. It has promised to be neutral, although it is hard to imagine that
any foxes will be consulted. "Hello Mr. Fox, my name is Janice and
I am currently doing a survey on hunting. You may be aware that it
is currently the custom to chase you and members of your family across
the English countryside for two hours before you are ripped apart by
a pack of dogs. Do you think ending this practice would (a) improve
your quality of life; (b) deny you the fun of the chase; or (c) make no
difference?" According to the pro-hunting Countryside Alliance most
foxes would shrug and answer "Er—'b' I s'pose."

If fox hunting is ultimately allowed to continue under new regulations then we should campaign to make these new rules as obstructive as possible. For a start, foxhounds must be kept on leads at all
times (though not those extendable ones that get wrapped around
everyone's legs). Harsh fines should be imposed for any hounds foul-
ing the footpaths, with the master of the hunt being made responsible for clearing up after his dogs. His little trumpet can be employed
to alert everyone that another dog is doing his business—that familiar fanfare will now mean, "Oh no, there's another one over here, pass
us another little polythene bag." Affirmative action must be taken
to ensure that minority breeds of dogs are not discriminated against,
forcing hunts to employ little shih tzus and miniature Chihuahuas,
who may need to be helped over some of the larger clumps of grass.

But anyone who believes that a compromise is really possible
should try explaining the Third Way to a fox. Either he gets ripped
to shreds or he doesn't. It is not a question of class warfare; hunting
should be banned because it is a matter of principle and of democ-

racy. The practice is barbaric, it's opposed by a huge majority of the British people, and the people who do it are a bunch of snobby Conservatives with stupid upper-class accents. Oh damn, I didn't say that, damn, what a giveaway . . .

Of course, this is really why fox hunting is so deeply unpopular. There is only one thing the English hate more than people being cruel to animals, and that is snooty rich people being cruel to animals. So why has the government apparently been dragging its feet on this issue? One moment it appears that the fox hunters face imminent abolition, then the government won't make time for a bill; then the PM gets them in his sights again, then there is going to be an inquiry. It's almost as if they have been deliberately stringing it out for as long as possible. Don't the fox hunters recognise these tactics? Can't they see that Labour is enjoying the thrill of the chase, that they are having political sport with country sports? Animal rights groups would like hunting killed off quickly and humanely, but that takes all the fun out of it. The pro-hunters are going to be hounded all the way up to the election. "Tally ho!" shouts Tony Blair as he sets off in his red jacket and riding hat, galloping after the fox hunters followed by packs of voters all baying for blood.

Because fox hunting is that most precious of political issues: one that unites his party, is popular in the country, will not be expensive to enact, and forces the leader of the opposition into an embarrassing and untenable position. There can be few sights that gladden hearts in Downing Street as much as that of the leader of the Conservative Party leading a march for the rights of posh people to be cruel to animals. Public opinion overwhelmingly demanded that fox hunting be abolished immediately. And that is why it wasn't.

So we can expect more marches to come. More fox hunters coming through our cities terrifying all the poor foxes who moved into town to get away from them. Obviously it's frustrating that hunting still goes on but there is something you can do until this Labour government finally delivers its promise. The next time there is a pro-hunting march through your city just grab one of the protesters, drag him down an alleyway, and nick his watch and his wallet. And when he protests just say to him, "You country folk; you just don't understand the ways of the city, do you?"

I GIVE YOU MY HEART (AND MY KIDNEYS AND PANCREAS)

21 March 2000

For years I have carried a kidney donor card in my wallet. Part of me wanted to scribble a couple of preconditions on the back of it, but the chances that any of my internal organs might be required by Mrs. Thatcher were so slight that I thought it not worth mentioning. However, now I learn that just carrying a donor card is often not enough; the hospital will still seek permission from my relatives. And unsurprisingly, breaking the news of someone's death and adding, "Oh, by the way, can we have his pancreas?" has sometimes proved a little awkward.

Different societies have found different solutions to the shortage of human organs for transplants. In China it is common practice to use the organs of executed prisoners. So every Chinese jail has a little counter where you can go in and say, "I'll have the number 47-A, please; two lungs, two corneas, and a liver." Then ten minutes later they come out of the back and pass over your order in a little white box.

Until recently, in India it was not only perfectly legal but also common practice for people to sell one of their kidneys when they needed to raise a little extra cash. They had a special section for it in the Indian newspaper small ads, between keyboards and kissograms. And if you were in need of expensive medical treatment you could do a part exchange; it was just a question of haggling. "Ooh no, I can't give you that much, I'm afraid . . ." the surgeon would say. ". . . You see, this kidney was originally one of a pair; it's not worth much without the other one."

"Oh well, I'd really like to hang on to one of them if it's all the same to you."

Hopefully nothing like this happens in Britain, although I have always been rather suspicious of those people who wear badges saying "Lose weight now, ask me how." Perhaps the British government might be tempted by the idea of selling kidneys on the open market. At last! A way for graduates to pay off their student loans!

In Belgium and Spain the shortage of organs is being tackled by a system that is termed "presumed consent." This means that there is a national register where you can specify that you do not wish any of your organs to be removed after your death. Otherwise it is assumed that you have no objection to saving someone else's life when your own is over. There are some people in Britain who would recoil at this idea; if you put a Belgian kidney in the body of a Conservative anti-European, the body would instinctively reject it. But now the British Medical Association has come out in favour of this system and is campaigning for a change in the law in the UK.

The problem with our system as it stands is that it is simply not working. Less than one in five people carry an organ donor card and the gap between demand and supply is growing all the time. Some hope that the shortfall will be made up by organs taken from animals, but this solution is still many years from being realised and brings its own problems. Will there be a choice of animal for the recipient? Will it be like choosing the fish in a French restaurant— "Er, I'll have the heart of that piglet there please . . ."? And I suppose it also raises the question, "Do animals have the ethical right to refuse their consent?" If I were a pig living in a pen marked "To be slaugh-tered for organ transplant" I think I might be quite keen to opt to join the register saying I'd rather not, thank you very much.

There are countless deaths every year caused by the unnecessary shortage of organs for transplant, and the government should have the courage to follow the advice of the BMA and change the law to presumed consent. Yes, it is a moral and ethical minefield, but if you weigh up the possible distress of a family who learned that their re-cently deceased son had his kidney removed before he was cremated, compared to the distress of the family who had to cremate their son because no organ could be found for a transplant, then it seems to me that the choice is clear. I, for one, would hope that if I lost one of my relations, doctors would not need to ask me if the internal organs could be used to help someone else. Although after last weekend, what with St. Patrick's Day and Ireland winning the rugby, I wouldn't wish my dad's liver on anybody.

WWW.OVER-HYPED.COM

24 March 2000

By common consent we are currently in the middle of a revolution. The Internet revolution differs slightly from the French and Russian revolutions in that rather than overthrowing the old world order in the quest for liberty and equality for all mankind, this revolution enables you to see what the weather's like in Ulan Bator without buying a newspaper. Bliss was it in that dawn to be alive.

This week, plans for a new Internet university were announced. It will be just like being at real university, except that everything will happen on your computer screen. There'll be a little traffic cone icon that you can pick up and drag back to your home page. There'll be a live chat page where you can make yourself a blobby coffee and stay up until three in the morning listening to the intellectual bloke talk about Italian renaissance painters, never daring to ask him why he keeps mentioning characters from *Teenage Mutant Ninja Turtles*. You will have immediate access to all the research material you need and e-mail with which to instantly return your work to your tutor; but all this will do is make it harder to come up with excuses as to why you are still two weeks late with your essay.

The electronic university is the latest headline in a long list of wonderful things that a computer and modem can do for mankind. There are e-bookshops where you can buy self-help guides to help you deal with the anxiety you felt ever since you divulged your credit card number over the Internet. There are virtual jobs in virtual offices where you go virtually mad never talking to another human being from one day to the next. Suddenly the Internet is the solution to everything. The prime minister is lying awake at night trying to think of a way forward for the peace process in Northern Ireland. "Have you thought about looking on the Internet?" asks Cherie. And obviously there it is, instantly available and all for the price of a local call. The way to end world poverty, the secret of eternal happiness, the cure for cancer—apparently you can find out anything from the Internet. The only problem is that when you enter the words "cure" and "cancer," your search engine will find four million sites, the first of which is the diary of a fifteen-year-old boy from Ottawa whose favourite band is The Cure and whose star sign is Cancer. And for some reason you find yourself reading ten pages about his trip to summer camp in British Columbia before you accept that this site isn't going to have the information you were looking for.

The usefulness of the Internet has been hyped out of all proportion. All it does is make information more easily available. The downside of this is that in doing so it creates an enormous amount of new material, most of which is just information for its own sake. Like mobile phone users on trains on the way to the office, loudly reporting that they are on a train and on their way to the office, much of what is posted on the Internet is up there because it *can* be, not because it *needs* to be. The medium is the message.

Clearly there are some specialist occupations for which the Internet is a vital resource, but since I am not a white supremacist with an interest in hard-core pornography, I find that most of the sites are not really for me. Knowledge is a wonderful thing, but for the time being I can survive without the latest major league water polo statistics delivered instantly to my e-mail address.

But imagine if a new craze suddenly came on the scene called "the library." Inside were these things called "books" about everything— encyclopedias, great works of literature, children's stories, manuals, history books, more reading material than you could ever hope to devour. And you could take these texts out of the library free because these "book" things were even more portable than a laptop, you could "read" them on the bus, in bed at night, anywhere. We would think it was the most fantastic development in the world. Yet today librar- ies are closing while funding for the Internet seems limitless. Is this because we have read all the books there are to read? No, it is simply that the Internet is new. It is so new that even the cynical British have failed to see that it is not a superhighway at all, but the infor- mation equivalent of Trafalgar Square at rush hour. In a few years' time things will be back to normal and we will all be complaining about how our favourite site on the World Wide Web takes ten sec- onds to access when it used to take only five, and telling our spoiled children that in our day we had to get the weather off the television. Then, at least, it will be useful—it will be something new for us to moan about. But in the meantime if you are one of the 80 percent of people in Britain who are not yet online, do not let all the hype make you believe you are missing out on something wonderful.

When people talk about "surfing" the Net you can rest assured that they are in fact comparing the Internet to the kind of surfing you get in North Cornwall. You spend a fortune on equipment, there's lots of hanging around for very little excitement, and every now and then something really disgusting bobs up to the surface.

AND THE AWARD FOR THE
BEST AWARDS CEREMONY ...

28 March 2000

Thiere were some fantastic actors up for an Oscar this year. You only had to look at the generosity of their smiles as they applauded the person who'd just beaten them to appreciate what brilliant performers they really are. The Oscars is without a doubt the biggest award ceremony in the world; somehow the knife-edge decision over who will get the Nobel Prize for Chemistry has failed to capture the public imagination in quite the same way.

Oscars night is now the occasion at which Western society honours its greatest heroes. In the old days celebrities didn't get awards; instead the pope would just create some more saints. At the annual sanctification dinner at the Vatican, Philip the Good would have to smile and applaud while inside he was spitting with jealousy that Joan of Arc had been made a saint while his Treaty of Arras had been completely overlooked by the judges.

Today there are awards ceremonies for virtually everything. For example, a friend of mine recently found himself attending the British Flooring Awards, which apparently saw great excitement as guests wondered who would win Best Adhesive-Backed Linoleum. Among the other genuine awards ceremonies that are held every night in the hotels along Park Lane are the Heating and Ventilation Awards, the Catering and Hotel Keeping Awards, and the Handling and Storage Awards. Perhaps there should be an awards ceremony for the best awards ceremony: "And the winner is *this awards ceremony!*"

More and more professions are realising that this is a way of raising their profile and keeping their workforces motivated. Soon hundreds of people will arrive at the Grosvenor House Hotel, suitably done out in stripey jumpers and eye masks, for the Burglar of the Year Awards. "My fellow burglars, this award doesn't belong to me . . ."

"Well no, Nobby, you just nicked it off Brian . . ."

Or live from Tehran, the International Terrorist Awards . . . "And the nominees are: Shining Path of Peru, Basque separatists, ETA, and the Animal Liberation Front!" And right across middle England, fingers will be crossed for that elusive British win, although just being nominated is in itself a great honor for the plucky animal lovers from Devon.

The problem with awards is when people start to take them seriously. Increasingly in the arts, prizes are taken as proof of merit. This year *American Beauty* won five Oscars so it is therefore a great film. But *The Straight Story* got nothing so it is not. In my opinion they are both excellent, but there's no objective way of measuring the best of anything in the arts. Nothing is definitely good and nothing is definitely bad—Jeffrey Archer's novels excepted.

Prizes for art and culture are of course part of a marketing scam just as much as they are in the heating and ventilation industry. In America at least they accept and understand this and no film that had completely bombed at the box office would be likely to win an Oscar. But in class-ridden Britain with all our snobbery and intellectual posturing the opposite is true; over here if a piece of culture is hugely popular it is presumed that it must automatically be rubbish. Art has to be difficult and inaccessible in order to be considered worthy of award status. If the Oscars were organised in the UK, the winner would be an obscure art film that nobody had liked or gone to see, but that got a few London film buffs very excited by its inversion of narrative form and the fact that everyone was talking in Esperanto.

So the next time the critics use the occasion of the Oscars to bemoan the lack of a British film industry, they should look to their own snobby prejudices that have helped separate the words "popular" and "culture." It is no surprise who gets the prize of all that British talent that is put into great films. A nervous hush falls across the room as the envelope is opened . . . "And the winner is . . . Hollywood!"

SNOBS' BORSTAL;
ONLY £15,000 A YEAR

4 April 2000

I f you live on one of those streets that are so posh they have residents' parking for their garbage cans, you may have noticed some strange children in your neighbourhood this week. Don't be alarmed; that couple unloading their new four-wheel drive don't make all their money by kidnapping children. Believe it or not, those kids are their own; they've just been to pick them up from boarding school.

This week, thousands of children will have returned to their "homes" for the first time since Christmas. They'll be seeing their pets, playing with their toys, sleeping in their own bedrooms, and for a few weeks experiencing something approaching normal family life. But just when they start to adjust, a few belongings will be packed into a trunk and they will be exiled to snobs' Siberia all over again. Whenever I worry that I may produce screwed-up kids, I console myself with the thought that at least I'm not spending thousands of pounds a year just to make really sure.

The fact that it is routine practise to separate children as young as seven from their parents should be a national scandal. Call the police, call social services—a child has been abandoned! Somehow it is unacceptable for a penniless refugee to keep her child with her as she begs on the street, but it's considered a social status symbol to be able to dump your children in a posh Borstal for eight months of the year. Call me a wet liberal but there is more to parenting than sending off a parcel containing a Dundee cake and a model airplane once every term.

Just as children who were beaten may themselves become violent parents, so Daddy will put his son down for his old school on the day that the poor child is born. I don't why these parents don't just dump the baby in a telephone box and have done with it. In Aztec society, children were occasionally sacrificed at the age of seven. On the given day, a child was taken to the top of the pyramid and then hurled to its death. And the Aztec dad pompously told his wife that it was for their child's own good while the mom tried to put a brave face on it by saying to herself, "Well they do have splendid cricket facilities in the Kingdom of the Sun God."

The range of activities they offer is the most common defence of these institutions. Well they may have more lacrosse pitches and their own theatre and a brand-new science lab and twelve computers for a class of twelve but without wanting to sound like a country-and-western song, what they don't have is *love*. When children are at boarding school there is no one there who loves them. There is nobody who will be on their side no matter what, and to whom they can just go to and cuddle whenever they feel like it. By sending away your children, you are separating them from the most important thing in their life, the most crucial factor in their development as fully rounded human beings. I have never understood why posh people always feel the need to possess so much stuff—horses, boats, holiday homes—yet when it comes to their own offspring they prefer to lease them on an occasional basis. Of course there are plenty of children who go to boarding school but may not be emotionally scarred. One of my best friends had a father in the Royal Air Force who was

constantly having to move and so from the age of eleven she shared
a dorm with eight other girls. She is one of the most balanced, warm-
hearted people I have ever met and, apart from the fact that she likes
the Carpenters, she does not seem to have been psychologically damaged in any way. But for every person like her there are countless dys-
functional adults who were denied proper role models, who have
problems communicating with the opposite sex, or worse, have grown
up believing that the Oxford versus Cambridge boat race is an interesting sporting event.

If you have just brought your children home and this is the first
you have seen of them since Christmas, don't take them back in four
weeks' time. Don't send them the subconscious message that you do
not want them around, that they are not welcome at home. Tell them
you love them so much you want to see them all year round. Tell
them you will undertake yourself to teach those important social skills
like talking too loudly and throwing bread rolls around in restaurants.
And think of the money you'll save; you can put it in a savings account for your children. They'll need it when the time comes to dump
you in an old people's home.

SO WHAT HAPPENED TO THE PEACE DIVIDEND?

11 April 2000

A momentous event took place over the weekend. A man from West Berkshire District Council took a pair of wire cutters and snipped through the fence surrounding Greenham Common. The former U.S. Air Force base, the old front line in the battle against nuclear weapons, is just an ordinary piece of common ground once more. It brings a patriotic lump to my throat. Now it can be used for more traditional English pastimes like scattering pornographic magazines about or pretending not to notice that your dog is going to the toilet.

I have seen firsthand the misery that nuclear weapons can cause. I once stood in the rain outside Greenham Common, holding hands with a peace studies lecturer from Bradford. But though the battle for the land has now been won, the principle for which so many women gave up their homes, jobs, and fashion sense has not. Britain still has nuclear weapons. And just as the peace camps have disappeared, so the issue has vanished from the British political agenda. The Cold War may be over, the world may have changed, but we are still spending billions on an independent deterrent that was originally "justified" on the grounds that it would prevent a Soviet attack on Western Europe. Today we could stop a Russian invasion by telling Triple A not to answer breakdown calls from any tanks west of Moscow.

So why does Britain still spend billions on nuclear weapons? The answer is, of course, for the same reason as before; it has nothing to do with military strategy and everything to do with political expediency. Because no political party dares to present the British electorate with the unpalatable truth that we are not an important enough country to warrant having the bomb. Ever since the end of World War II the British have been living under a massive self-delusion about our relative significance as a world player and key to this has been our possession of nuclear weapons. We have been like a family struggling to make ends meet in a housing project in the West Midlands. As they sink deeper into debt the wife tentatively suggests to her husband, "Well, we could always get rid of the yacht . . ."

"Get rid of the yacht? Are you mad?"

"But it's costing us a fortune, dear, and we don't sail or live by the sea or anything . . ."

"But what would the neighbours think of us if we didn't have a yacht? We'd be a laughingstock."

There are plenty of things that we believed in the 1950s that we now realise are simply not true. The Royals are not the perfect family unit, the police are not always 100 percent honest, and *Gumby and Friends* was not a hilarious tour de force. But the British people still cling to the idea that Britain is a major military power and so no politician dares suggest we give up our nuclear weapons. We might all be driving around in German and Japanese cars, but hey, we've got the bomb and they haven't. There must be cheaper ways of making ourselves feel superior to the Germans. Practising for penalty shoot-outs for the World Cup would be a start.*

---

*On more than one occasion England has been knocked out of a major soccer tournament after losing a penalty shoot-out to the Germans. I suppose we should be grateful that this system wasn't used to decide the outcome of two world wars.

In fact the billions that we have spent over the years on our nuclear white elephant is partly the reason why we have less economic clout than many of our neighbours. Imagine if some of that money had gone into education and industry? What use are atom bombs when BMW closes Rover; we can't nuke Munich, even if there are some in the Conservative Party who would argue otherwise. This week it was reported that Britain would actually need several days to get its missiles ready to fire. Presumably that's the time it would take for the U.S. president to return Britain's phone message asking for permission. In a parliamentary answer the defence secretary revealed that Britain's cash-strapped nuclear submarines were on a reduced state of alert in order that they could concentrate on "secondary tasks." In other words, *"Trips around the lighthouse £1; children 50p."*

Our Trident submarines could never fire their missiles independently of an American military operation. So it makes no more sense for Britain to spend billions to have its own deterrent than it would for the state of North Dakota. We are part of a military alliance completely dominated by Washington; our "independent" deterrent is in fact just part of the American nuclear arsenal, the only catch being that we have to pay for it. Perhaps that's why it's called a "special relationship." Though the United States will always be a nuclear power, today there is less reason than ever for Britain to live in penury so that we can keep paying our subscriptions to be a member of the nuclear club. The bomb is an irrelevant status symbol from another age. It's like those platform shoes that we all wore in the '70s. We felt great because they made us feel so tall. It was just a shame they prevented us from doing anything useful like walking.

WHY WAS MOTHER NATURE A SINGLE MUM?

17 April 2000

The specialization of in vitro fertilization, frozen embryos, and human fertility is a very sensitive ethical issue and is not a subject for cheap jokes and smutty innuendo. But here goes anyway. . . .

The recent announcement that frozen eggs may be released for conception has major implications for the future of family planning. Women will now be able to freeze their own eggs and keep them for later use, unless of course the freezer breaks down and they have to rush round to their next-door neighbour's with the contents of their ovaries pressed between a packet of frozen peas and some McCain oven chips. The eggs will of course come with their own "fertilize by" date. Three stars on the side of the packet above where it says Best Before Jan 2010.

The next stage takes place in a special building where people spend all day aiming frozen sperm in the general direction of frozen eggs, which all sounds rather like an unheated student house in Scotland I once stayed in. Successful fertilization can take some time, but when you have five billion sperm to choose from you can't expect Ms. Egg to make her mind up right away. One of the more bizarre objections I have heard to IVF is that there is no love in the act of conception. As if the test tube should take the woman out to dinner first, go back for coffee, and say, "You're so much more than just a friend . . ."

The voices that normally oppose every development in fertility treatment have been reluctant to criticise a decision that will give the chance of motherhood to women who have become infertile through cancer treatment. But—shock, horror, and hold the front page—this ruling will also allow women to freeze eggs until they choose to have babies later in life for personal or social reasons.

There is an unspoken assumption that because women's fertility falls away at around the time that they reach forty, they must be less suitable as potential mothers. That reduced egg production is just nature's way of making sure that babies get the best mothers. Well, on this occasion, nature has got it wrong. Nature makes it easier for a woman to get pregnant when she is fourteen than when she is forty, so what does Mother Nature know? And anyway, what happened to "Father Nature"—maybe she should have chosen someone who was going to stick around before she started laying down the rules for all the other mums.

It is not fair that women should have to put up with worrying about their ability to have babies as they head toward forty. If we are allowed to use contraception to plan our families, then why not developments in technology? Imagine if the history of human fertility had been the other way around. That the only way to conceive a child was to plan and time your pregnancy using cryotechnology. And then a new potion was developed called "Martini and soda," which when drunk all night increased your chances of getting pregnant in the back of the van of the bloke who ran the mobile disco. We would think the new system was complete madness. Babies produced through accidents, babies produced randomly to couples who didn't want them . . . this is what happens at the moment, thousands of babies are conceived in Britain every year, none of them to perfect parents, many of them unplanned and born into families that will struggle to raise them. That's fine; most parents will rise to the challenge and give their children all the love and support that their circumstances allow. But to say that somehow a woman who wants to wait till she's found someone who'll be a really good father, or until she feels she has the financial security that a new baby needs, that these mothers are crossing a line of moral unacceptability is clearly bonkers.

As ever the opposition to this comes from the religious right. A number of church leaders have expressed opposition to IVF though half of them probably thought they were being quizzed about some terrorist organization. No doubt at some point in the Bible it clearly states, "Thou shalt not have thy seed put in liquid nitrogen, nor shall the eggs of woman be cryogenically stored till she hath found her Mr. Right through the computer dating agency, verily." But the reason they instinctively oppose this new development is that deep down the church does not like change. They are still sulking from being proved wrong about the sun going around the earth and frankly they've been struggling to keep up ever since. But I like to think that Jesus would have had sympathy with women who wanted to bring children into this world when they were best placed to cope with them. Why am I so confident that our Lord would have been in favour of test-tube babies? The religious conservatives should stop and think about it for a moment. Who was the first-ever baby to be produced through IVF? Why, Jesus Christ himself, of course.

CHARITY BEGINS A LONG
WAY FROM HOME

20 April 2000

Y ou could tell which people were running the London Marathon for charity. They were the ones carrying plywood Spanish galleons strapped over their shoulders. "In aid of theBritish Heart Foundation" said their T-shirts as they lay wheezing on the road side while St. John's Ambulance checked to see if they'd given themselves a coronary.

For some reason it has become the accepted convention that people raising money for charity are compelled to dress up in stupid costumes. Why is it that giving up time or money also requires us to surrender our dignity at the same time? "Thousands are starving in Ethiopia so I'm going to sit in a bath full of baked beans and do a sponsored singathon of ABBA hits." The Bible does not say what Jesus was wearing at the feeding of the five thousand, but I can't imagine he dressed up as a pantomime dame and stuffed two balloons under his shirt while all the Romans looked on with a smile, saying "It's all right, it's for charity . . ."

Perhaps being madcap and bonkers is a way of coping with the awfulness of the suffering to which we are drawing attention. Occasionally, as with the current crisis in Ethiopia, the problems seem so huge that we just want to put them out of our heads altogether. We pretend we're doing enough for charity by buying a lottery ticket, and reassure ourselves that if we won the jackpot we'd give a lot more.

The fact is that most of us won the lottery on the day that we were born. We rubbed the little silver bit on the scratch card of fate and it came up with "Middle Class, Western Society" and we punched the air and shouted "Yes!" The bloke next to us rubbed his coin onto his scratch card and saw that he'd got "Peasant, Horn of Africa." "Oh, bad luck, mate. I might as well take that coin off you before you go."

But despite our enormous good fortune some of us are still reluctant to give a little of our comparative wealth away. This might be because we have an aversion to medical students collecting for rag week dressed as characters from *South Pacific*. But it is more likely that we have a deep-seated fear that we may be taken for a ride, that we may be giving a pound that won't get to its intended destination. But isn't this a risk worth taking? Even if it was true (which it is certainly not) that only a fraction of third world aid gets through to those who really need it, a mere ten pence would still be worth much more to the intended recipient than the original pound was to us. In fact with emergency relief every penny generally goes straight to the famine-hit areas. The Red Cross, for example, is currently running daily flights carrying maize and soya directly into the worst-hit areas (the airline food stays on the plane; the Ethiopians have already suffered enough). The Oxfam fact sheet in front of me says that £2 buys enough seed to plant a whole acre of sorghum in the Sudan. This is an incredible fact. Okay, I don't actually know what sorghum is, it could be local slang for cannabis for all I know, but it still sounds like a bargain. What else can you get for two measly quid? Seven minutes' parking in central London. A disappointingly small packet of cashew nuts. One unfunny greeting card. My kids are currently stuffing their faces with an Easter egg that cost £3. The same amount could pay for a girl in Bangladesh to go to school for three months. Admittedly the girl in Bangladesh would much rather have the big chocolate Easter egg but that's beside the point.

Yet many people will give to "good causes" only if they can personally witness the benefits of their own largesse. In reality the good cause is their own ego. A friend of mine showed me his latest copy of the magazine sent to alumni of Westminster School. It proudly reported that a former pupil has just given one million pounds to his old private school. "Hmmm . . ." this old boy must have thought. "Who can I think of that really needs a million quid? Starving Ethiopians, maybe? Flood victims in Mozambique? Children with leukemia? No!" he decided. "Clearly it has to be Westminster School, where all those poor children of millionaire merchant bankers and Conservative politicians are currently having to get by with Internet access limited to off-peak hours only." What more deserving cause could there be?

But unless thousands of emaciated refugees are massing on the cricket pitches of your old private school, I urge you to make a donation to Ethiopian famine relief now. Don't make excuses to yourself; nothing but good can come out of any donation you make. Remember, £1 keeps distress at bay for a whole day, £10 will pay for a whole week of smugness, £50 guarantees a whole year of sanctimoniously refusing other charities. So ring that helpline now. And remember this is for charity, so don't forget to put on your Elvis costume before you make that call.

ANARCHY AND APATHY
IN THE UK

2 May 2000

Millions of homes in Britain will have recently received an electoral registration card. These have a variety of uses: you can put them by the phone and use them to scribble down numbers; you can fold them and stick them under wobbly tables; or you can tear them up and use them for making joints. If you are really adventurous you might actually use yours to go and vote this week, although tragically you would be in the minority.

Participation in British elections is bad and getting worse. At the last Euro elections the turnout was so low that when a candidate asked for a recount the returning officer said "All right then—okay, I've finished!" Perhaps there should be more incentive to go and vote, a *Reader's Digest*–type prize for the person who turns up with the lucky magic polling number. Since the main political parties feel compelled to offer bribes at election time, I sometimes wonder why they don't just have done with it and stand outside the polling station shouting "Vote Conservative and get two hundred pounds cash, a new DVD, and a night out with the Spice Girls."

The sad truth is that people don't value the fantastic prize that has already been won for them—the right to vote. It is only within the lifetime of many older voters that we have obtained universal suffrage in the United Kingdom, and yet when our polling cards land on the doormat, we regard them with about as much respect as minicab cards and the leaflet from Speedy Pizzas. The suffragette Emily Davison lost her life jumping in front of the king's horse at the 1913 Derby so that we could live in a democracy. Maybe that wasn't her motive; maybe she just had a pound to win on the horse that was running second. At this very moment there are people in jail for the crime of advocating democracy. They dreamt of a society in which every citizen had the right to vote. As a member of Amnesty International I have sent postcards to such political prisoners, though I decided it probably wouldn't be very tactful to tell them we'd achieved their vision of utopia over here, but found that people generally prefer to stay in and watch *Friends* on a Thursday evening.

There are all sorts of reasons why people feel that it's not worth bothering to struggle down to the polling station. One reason is that most people still have very little power over their own lives; they feel excluded by society and so turn their backs on the narrow choices offered to them. This is not a symptom of a failure of democracy per se, but of a democracy still in its infancy. And when our "democratic" society fails to live up to its promise, the reaction varies wildly from apathy to the anarchy we saw in the cities around the world yesterday.

I had been completely unaware that there was such a strong groundswell of feeling against the World Trade Organization. But now I actually feel rather ashamed that I'm not doing anything about the destruction of the planet or the increasing poverty in the third world. I did do one bit of campaigning last year, lobbying my local councilors on an issue close to my heart. It was successful too, and our street got speed humps soon afterward. But somehow the overthrow of global capitalism just seems like a slightly bigger fish.

Although I think that the increasing sense of powerlessness in citizens of the undemocratic global economy was a factor in this week's violence, seeing the bloke next to you get his head smashed open by a police baton must also be a factor. I have been on enough marches and protests to know how violence erupts. There is a symphonic narrative to a demonstration. It begins quietly—a gentle stroll with a few light diversions along the way, such as the vision of the statue of a nineteenth-century statesman holding a placard saying "I'm gay and I'm proud. Abolish Clause 28." Eventually the symphony enters its second movement as the chanting begins. It is led by someone with a cheap megaphone, so distorted that you cannot tell what it is you are shouting about. He might well be screaming "The opposite of 'In' is . . ." and you all reply "Out! Out! Out!"

Then the march reaches its destination and its climax. A tense standoff begins in which a bunch of young blokes in jeans and T-shirts wait around to find out what will happen if they shout insults at a line of policemen in full riot gear. The police may well be on the receiving end of the odd improvised light missile, but bits of plywood stick broken off the Socialist Worker Party banners are unlikely to pierce a line of reinforced riot shields. But that is all the provocation that is needed before the order comes down: "Send in the Overreaction Squad!" These are officers that have spent months at Police College training how to completely overreact to perfectly containable situations. Those who do not act with extreme and unnecessary violence are told they don't make the grade. If they respond to this news by tipping up the desk and punching their senior officer in the face then they are back in again.

When the police charge a crowd of demonstrators anyone is generally fair game. This is the moment when a jolly day out turns into a scene of ugly and upsetting violence. On one demo I remember seeing an old hippie who would clearly never hurt anyone being felled by the baton of a policeman in full riot gear. One moment he is telling everyone to cool it, the next he has blood pouring down the front of his face and he's crying from shock and frustration and you don't feel like cooling it at all, you feel an enormous anger that makes you want to hit back at the idiots who could do such a thing to a harmless bloke who just went on a march because he wanted to make the world a better place. With one stupid piece of indiscriminate violence the police manage to turn us all into an angry spitting mob.

As a general rule the genuinely ugly violence on demonstrations is started by the police. A few years back there was an attempt by some German police officers to discover who really started the trouble and they infiltrated a demo disguised as protesters. They got their answer when they were set upon by several uniformed policemen and beaten senseless. Of course there are always a handful of demonstrators who go looking for violence, but that doesn't mean that anyone has to give it to them.

In this era of reconciliation I am surprised that Bill Clinton and Tony Blair have not made any effort to bring the police and eco-warriors closer together. Batons should not be made from tropical hardwoods but from trees grown in sustainable forests. More effort should be made to recruit officers with big metal studs through their eyelids. For their part eco-warriors should spend a month working out in the police gym and then be kitted out with a macho black padded uniform and riot shield with extra long baton. The temptation to whack someone in a clown costume doing circus acts must be quite strong.

But for now it seems depressingly inevitable that these protests will end in violence. On Monday night the situation forced Railtrack to close Euston Station as pitched battles were fought between police and rioters, vehicles were set alight, and the mob wreaked havoc in their protests against global capitalism and world poverty. And then at last the silent apathetic majority who can't even be bothered to vote anymore found that they too had something to be angry about.

"Honestly!" they tutted to themselves, "What excuse will the railway companies come up with next?"

The anticapitalists who now regularly choose to celebrate May Day by getting smashed over the head with a police truncheon will cease to be a fringe novelty unless political power becomes genuinely devolved from the center and people are routinely involved in decisions that affect their lives, nationally and locally and in their workplaces. The alternative to real democracy in which people feel it is worth their while going out to vote is a society in which political opposition is regularly expressed with rioting, looting, and throwing custard pies in Bill Gates's face. It is not a pretty sight. And the custard pie doesn't help either. Violence against individuals or world capitalism cannot be the way to construct a fairer, more democratic society. Tempting though it might be to vent our anger by hitting out at the symbols of the establishment, the only way forward must be to try to make the world a better place through the existing political system. We have sufficient freedom to go on and achieve real freedom, as Trotsky said to his friend with the ice pick. Democracy is a precious and fragile thing and we cannot allow it to be threatened by anarchy or apathy. But just in case you disagree, Bill Gates lives in Seattle and custard pies are available in most good bakeries in the area.

SHIP OF FOOLS

13 May 2000

They have given up trying to find the Lost City of Atlantis. The unpaid city tax has been written off, the telephone code remains unchanged, and Atlantis will soon have to surrender its city status to either Brighton or Inverness. But now someone has finally come up with a replacement. Across the Atlantic, work is beginning on the construction of the world's first floating city: a huge oceangoing society with permanent residential accommodation for 40,000 people, with its own schools, hospitals, offices, and of course, shopping malls. The entrepreneurs behind the "Freedom Ship" believe that thousands of people will buy "properties" and then live and work on this seaborne city; that they will run businesses and bring up families while the giant vessel sails endlessly back and forth between the hottest parts of the world in search of sun, sea, and skin cancer.

It is *Brave New World* meets *The Flying Dutchman*—except that Wagner would probably have been a bit liberal for the residents of the Freedom Ship. The name itself immediately marks out the project as deeply suspect—the word "Freedom" with a capital F is generally used only by nutty right-wing organizations and the makers of sanitary napkins. The liberty to which it refers is of course freedom from taxes—the ship will be an enormous floating tax haven—like the Cayman Islands, but without the radical edge. In fact the "Freedom" Ship will be a dictatorship run by the captain, but who cares about that when all the alcohol is duty-free, when you are on the world's longest booze cruise.

The project's promotional material does everything it can to suggest that a life at sea is a healthy one, but there is more to health than a bit of sun, a gymnasium, and a few cycle lanes. There is your mental health and nothing is more guaranteed to drive you off your head than living forever in a society made up entirely of the people you met on holiday. Apparently the ship will boast a multilanguage library—so you can choose between Dick Francis in English or German. The website does not mention whether this particular city will have a red light district, but since they're hoping that entrepreneurs will start up their own businesses on board and they are promising extensive landscaping you might keep your eyes open by those bushes behind the tennis courts.

The really fascinating thing about the Freedom Ship is what it tells us about the psychology of those who seek to establish a capitalist utopia by starting all over again somewhere else. They think that society's problems have nothing to do with them; that the unpleasant experiences of people begging, stealing, or charging them VAT are random bits of bad luck that have happened because of their postal address. They imagine that you can leave all human ills behind in the same way that you can sail away from cold weather. The project is a logical progression from those high-security private housing developments with electric gates and CCTV—private solutions to social problems for which we are all responsible. The Freedom Ship will apparently be such a perfect society that they are going to have one security officer for every twenty residents. How reassuring: being stuck on a boat with two thousand bored private security guards made up of failed policemen and sacked bouncers who needed to get away from their own countries in a hurry.

The marketing material also boasts that thanks to a unique system of separate tanks, the world's largest ship will be completely unsinkable. Which is a great line but one I'm sure I've heard before somewhere—I think it was followed by Kate Winslet nodding nervously and noticing how few lifeboats there were. Apparently the vessel is so large and stable that you wouldn't know that you are at sea. So it's worth all that effort then.

If the Freedom Ship doesn't sink it will probably be captured by Indonesian pirates or there will be a mutiny by passengers driven insane by years spent watching CNN and playing quoits. But you can be sure that something will go wrong because the words "capitalist" and "utopia" are incompatible. That's not to say that some form of perfect society is not possible because after the launch I really can foresee it. Imagine a city ship floating around on the other side of the world with all the shallow, tax-dodging, soulless, right-wing, cruise ship customers permanently on board. Of course it would be a living hell—it would be the worst society imaginable. But wouldn't it be paradise back here without them?

GAWD BLESS YER, MA'AM

17 May 2000

The government has announced that it is to charge £500 to guests wishing to attend the Queen Mother's hundredth birthday party. It's a desperate measure but it's the only way they could be sure of keeping Fergie away. Of course £500 is only for starters; guests will be even more out of pocket by the time they're sorted for E's and wizz.

The Conservatives are outraged about this vulgar plan to claw back some of the cost of the celebrations; they praised the Queen Mother as "a long-established institution," which sounds as if they may have been mixing her up with Strangeways Borstal. The Royalist Right had barely recovered from the front page headline "How dare the BBC snub the Queen Mother," under which a corporation that is usually lambasted for screening dull unpopular programmes was criticised for not filming a few soldiers marching around Horse Guards Parade being waved at. If it was such a great programme Rupert Murdoch would have bought the rights ages ago.

The BBC will be criticised whatever they do. Way back in 1923 the progressives were angry that there was no radio broadcast of the wedding of Elizabeth Bowes-Lyon (as she was then known) to the Duke of York. This was refused because it was feared (and I'm not making this up) "that disrespectful people might hear it whilst sitting in pubs with their hats on." God forbid that anything so discourteous should come to pass today, although the Eleven O'Clock Show's photomontage of the Queen Mum's head on a naked pensioner's body must come close.

In providing a completely pointless thing about which to be outraged, the Queen Mother is of course fulfilling her historic duty. The reason that she has been built up to untouchable iconic status is so that subscribers to *Majesty* magazine have something to tut about when we say she is "lovely" only five times over instead of the statutory twenty-seven. The BBC is actually spending a million quid covering her one-hundredth birthday, which sounds like plenty and if it's any consolation somebody might point out to her that they definitely intend to provide live coverage of her funeral. And the government is in fact spending £400,000 on the celebrations, which is more than most pensioners have managed to get out of it recently. But still the Conservatives are furious at the lack of enthusiasm. This week they criticised British involvement in Sierra Leone on the grounds that the army might not have sufficient manpower to carry out more important duties elsewhere. Now we know to what they were referring. Never mind preventing genocide; we need the army band back here to play "Happy Birthday." All sorts of other festivities are planned. For example, one royal press release announced that on 2 June in St. Paul's Cathedral, the Princess Royal "will unveil the bust of the Queen Mother," which is not an image you want to dwell upon. On 12 April she was presented with citizenship of Volgograd (formerly Stalingrad) for her work for that heroic city during the war. Although I have read *Stalingrad* I must have missed the chapter in which she led a Soviet tank division and isolated von Paulus's Sixth Army from the rest of the Third Reich.

Of course The War is the reason why it is outright treason not to love the Queen Mum. As we have been told a thousand times, she opted not to go abroad during the blitz even after her home received a direct hit, only half a mile from her bedroom. To reflect this, her birthday celebrations include a fly-past of World War II aircraft (which will then fly over the channel for a re-enactment of the bombing of Dresden). This is all part of the attempt to portray her as an ordinary patriotic citizen who toughed it out during Britain's darkest hour with all the other cockneys. The really popular superstar royals, like the Queen Mother and Diana, are not royals at all, but have merely married one—and these icons are served up as one of us. "I mean your Queen Mum, she was just born in an ordinary castle, weren't she, I mean she's not posh like the rest of 'em, is she; look at her mum and dad—ordinary working-class geezers, they were, old Lord Claude Bowes-Lyon and Cecilia Cavendish-Bentinck."

Personally I cannot get excited about an elderly aristocrat's birthday, and if it were down to me the celebrations would be even more low-key. The important thing with old people is not to put them under too much stress. What could be worse than organising a hundredth birthday extravaganza and having her die in the middle of it all? Perhaps they should cancel those plans for the Full Monty show live at the Palace.

What is completely bizarre is that a huge section of the British population still apparently feels such enormous love for someone about whom they know so little. She may have a nice smile and an ability to wave, but then so have the cartoon characters walking round Disneyland. Oh no, I've just had a terrible thought. A hundred-year-old lady that we never hear speak, who waves out a big carriage? No wonder she never died, it's just someone inside a foam Queen Mother costume, one of the chief attractions to the Great Britain–land theme park. How could we have been so gullible!

KEEP THE PINK FLAG FLYING

2 June 2000

've just read a leaflet in which homosexuality was portrayed as normal and acceptable and that was enough for me, I've suddenly decided to become gay. One brief glance at some mildly tolerant literature has forced me to leave my wife and kids and henceforth I shall have to spend my weekends browsing around Harrods' soft furnishings department and watching old Judy Garland movies.

This is what happens in the minds of those who oppose the repeal of Clause 28. That if you do not condemn homosexuality as an ungodly perversion every time it is mentioned, then children will automatically become gay and run around the playground going "Urrggghh! Bazza kissed a girl, Bazza is straight—he's a bloody hetero!" The idea that propaganda can reverse your sexuality is patently ridiculous. Every day in our society we are constantly exposed to aggressively heterosexual propaganda and it doesn't make Boy George decide to become a scaffolder so that he can leer at passing young women. We are what we are: gay, straight, or Rock Hudson through my mother's eyes.

But then we have the launch of a media campaign in Scotland to prevent Clause 28's overdue removal from the statute books as the

leader of the Catholic church in Scotland, Cardinal Thomas Winning, described homosexuality as a perversion. Gay rights campaigners angrily condemned his remarks, saying "Oooh, get her!"

Clause 28 was one of the madder pieces of legislation to have been
rushed through Parliament during the Thatcher years. It was a law
that the right-wing tabloids effectively wrote by proxy after they seized
upon an innocent specialized book called *Jennie Lives with Eric and
Martin*, which apparently demonstrated everything that was wrong
with loony Labour authorities. The book was in fact only used in rare
cases where children were being brought up by gay male couples, but
according to the religious right impressionable youngsters were being
forced to become homosexual. School assemblies had been abandoned and in their place kids were being compelled to wear leather
motorcycle caps and listen to Madonna records. The eating of quiche
was made compulsory. "School outings" took on a completely different meaning.

Soon the outcry reached fever pitch; Conservative MPs were furious that ordinary school children were being exposed to homosexuality when they themselves had to spend a fortune in boarding school
fees for the same privilege. And so a law was passed making it illegal
for local councils to promote homosexuality as normal or "acceptable." Which means of course that unless schools were going to completely deny the existence of homosexuality, they were legally bound
to describe it as *unacceptable*. English teachers were obliged by law
to say things like "The set book for this term is *The Ballad of Reading
Gaol*, which Oscar Wilde wrote while he was in prison for being a
disgusting queer and quite right too, the filthy pervert should have
been flogged as well, except he probably would have enjoyed it."

But since this regressive law was passed in the mid-eighties, something unexpected and wonderful has happened. Homosexuality has
become accepted. Suddenly there are openly gay ministers, even gay

Conservatives, and generally people don't care anymore. Celebrities pose for family newspapers with their gay partners. A few years ago this would have been inconceivable. The change of atmosphere has been hastened by legal steps taken by this government in its first couple of years in office. The age of consent for gays has been lowered, gay male couples have won joint parental rights, and the ban on gays in the army has been repealed. "Gay sailors!" said the opponents. "Whatever next! Homosexuals in the British secret service?" Of course there is still too much homophobia in our society; there are still gay-bashers who feel they are given a legitimacy by the likes of Cardinal Winning. But the campaign in Scotland will fail for the same reason that Clause 28 was completely misconceived. You cannot change anyone's sexuality with a book and you cannot throw £500,000 worth of leaflets at an issue and hope that it will turn back the tide of tolerance that has been coming for years. Instead there should be a new piece of legislation—call it Section 29—which makes it an offence to incite hatred against minorities. If these homophobic Scottish Conservatives weren't such a ridiculous minority themselves, this might not be such a bad idea. Labour must have the courage of their convictions and see through the abolition of Clause 28 north of the border. And instead of trying to defuse the row, they should use their powers to punish Cardinal Winning for being such a bigot. Then at mass on Sunday the leader of the Catholic church in Scotland will be forced to announce "And now we will sing hymn number 299, 'YMCA' by the Village People." Kissing the bishop's ring will never be the same again.

THE WAR IS OVER

7 June 2000

This week is the anniversary of the D day landings. Last week it was the anniversary of the evacuation of Dunkirk. Next week is probably the anniversary of the release of *Pearl Harbor* and Prince Charles will unveil a memorial to all those actors who died on the set. In Britain there is always a reason to look back at the Second World War. One of these days an explorer is going to land on this island and shout "The war is over!" and everyone will come blinking out from the undergrowth where we've been hiding in our tatty uniforms since 1945. As far as the British people are concerned, the history of Planet Earth goes like this: (1) The earth cools. (2) Primitive life-forms emerge. (3) Britain wins World War II. Apart from that nothing much of any importance has happened, with the possible exception of England winning the World Cup and the Beatles going on the Ed Sullivan show.

Anniversaries are a way of cherry-picking our history and avoiding the complex and sometimes unpalatable truth. For example this year is the hundredth anniversary of the end of the Boer War but where are the celebrations of Britain's invention of the concentration camp? There ought to be pages about it in the *Daily Telegraph*.

"Typical! Britain invents something and then the Germans and Japanese go and do it better than us!"

When we do focus on a piece of our history it is not to better understand it, but to mythologize it yet further. Why is it that we still cling to the legend of Dunkirk? Perhaps because it is the only time in our history that we have got to the beaches before the Germans. My father was at Dunkirk; while thousands were fighting to get on a ferry, he was the one looking for the duty-free shop. It is understandable that men of his generation still see the war as the defining experience of their lives. But what depresses me is seeing the twenty-something English football fans being interviewed in the run-up to the European football championship whose perceptions of mainland Europe are still based on a distorted history of the Second World War. "Well Britain, like, stood alone, against Hitler and Colonel Klink who wanted BMW to buy out all the British car factories and I'm really proud of how Britain stopped the Nazis and that we're all going to invade Holland and Belgium, give the fascist salute and beat up loads of foreigners."

Like much of the popular understanding of World War II, our interpretation of Dunkirk is a triumph of spin. As in any war the real story is complex and chaotic. But the British army was not rescued by an armada of little pleasure boats; 300,000 English soldiers did not come back across the channel on pedalos. The British army was in fact saved by a gross tactical error by Adolf Hitler, who halted his generals when they were on the verge of capturing the entire British army. He then went on to increase our chances of survival yet further by invading Russia and declaring war on the United States. His generals were furious with him but decided that he wasn't the sort of bloke to whom you could say "You've really cocked up big time here, Adolf."

It was necessary at the time to build up the symbolism of little Englanders standing up to the German Wehrmacht, but by allowing the myth to endure and grow we have done ourselves nothing but harm. Britain standing alone in 1940 was the consequence of a military disaster in which it failed to prevent the fall of France—it is not the basis for anti-European foreign policy sixty years later. Furthermore, by distorting our historical status and pretending that we fought World War II all on our own, we have inevitably created a sense of frustration when Britain then consistently fails to dominate the world in politics and sports in the way that we've been encouraged to believe that it's our right to do. The backlash then comes at events like the Euro 2000 soccer finals.

So stand on the white cliffs of Dover and wave off the little ships as they sail off to Dunkirk to re-enact Britain's finest hour. But leave the boats over there for a week or two, because we're going to need them to bring back all the disgraced English football fans. And then the news reporters will ask "Why is it that these thugs hate the German supporters so much?" before they head off to film the next anniversary of a war that ended more than half a century ago.

MICROSOFT WORLD

14 June 2000

ncluded free with Windows 2000 will be a computerised edition of the game "Monopoly." In this version Microsoft already owns every single property and you just go round and round giving them lots of money. You try to tell yourself it's not fixed but when Bill Gates wins second prize in a beauty competition you can't help being suspicious.

Over the past two years, in a legal battle even more difficult to understand than the Microsoft user's manual, the computer giant has been found guilty of anticompetitive practises and abusing its monopoly of power. Considering how aggressively Microsoft has consistently stamped on any competition their lawyers really should have seen this lawsuit coming, but then this is the company whose computers failed to foresee that the year 2000 would follow 1999, so you can't presume anything. Now an American judge has ordered Gates to spell out in detail how he is going to break up his company, which should certainly provide a challenge. Bill Gates talking at length about computer software and financial law; the last one in the courtroom left awake is the winner.

Since losing the case Gates has seen his personal wealth drop by around 25 billion dollars, so he's had to postpone buying that second car he and his wife had been saving up for. Internet Explorer will probably no longer be given free with Windows, which means that poor Internet users like me will end up having to pay more to write reviews of our own books on *amazon.co.uk*. It is of course true that Microsoft has stifled competition, but just a moment, who is it that is saying that this sort of behaviour is unacceptable? The United States government! This would be like Gates telling Clinton he's a bit nerdy. There are a number of monopolies in this world but the United States has a monopoly on all of them. Of course, this case is not really about free trade. It is a battle between the world's most powerful country and the world's most powerful company. It is the first flashpoint in the new cold war between nation-states and corporations. More battles between the giants will follow: Japan versus Sony, Korea versus Daewoo, Britain versus Twinings Tea. America won the first Cold War on behalf of capitalism. And what thanks do they get? Capitalism then proceeds to push America aside and the next struggle ensues.

Bill Gates should now hit back by countersuing the United States for operating anticompetitive practises. He would have a very good case. As a government, the United States has consistently stifled free trade. Tiny independent operators like Venezuela and Nicaragua have been virtually forced out of business and all sorts of international laws broken in the process. With the kind of breathtaking arrogance that you get only from the leaders of world superpowers and seventeen-year-old private school boys, America actually attempted to make it illegal for European countries to trade with Cuba; the case against America is even greater than the one against its richest citizen. Like Microsoft, the U.S. government has a variety of operating systems; in the Balkans it used NATO, but the World Trade Organization, the World Bank, and even the United Nations itself have all been called into play at various times to ensure that the odds are always stacked in favour of American commercial interests. This will probably be the last European Football Championship in which a team from Europe is allowed to win.

Any fair-minded judge would have to agree that like Microsoft, the United States has abused its monopoly of power and must therefore be broken up. It has refused to operate a level playing field and so must be separated into its constituent parts. Dividing it between North and South is one option but this was apparently tried before and caused all sorts of problems. You could split it between Democrats and Republicans or Pepsi and Coke drinkers or between the pro- and anti-gun lobbies, though this might be a bit unfair if another civil war broke out. But the American courts have ruled that monopolies should not be allowed to dominate and so the United States must be as good as its word. If Microsoft Windows is not allowed to give you free bundled software, then each Americanised country should not automatically get a McDonald's in every High Street and Jenny Jones repeats on their TV channels.

There must be a way of dividing America up so that the rest of the world could continue to get all the great bits without the stuff it would rather stayed at home. Can we have *The Simpsons* but not have Fox? Can we have the films without having to watch the acceptance speeches at the Oscars? Can we have the music without the graffiti on our subways? The breakup of America will be such a complex job that somebody will have to design a computer program to do it. If only Microsoft hadn't been fragmented. It probably had a free program on Windows 2000 that could have done it all for us.

A MIDSUMMER'S NIGHT DOME

21 June 2000

Today is the summer solstice and the most important date in the calendar for pagans, druids, and the man who tears off the little tickets at the Stonehenge car park. For as long as anyone can remember Stonehenge has been witness to an ancient midsummer ceremony in which hippies try to approach the stone circles and are then ritually whacked over the head by policemen in traditional riot gear. This year, however, with a callous disregard toward our prehistoric customs, English Heritage has opened up the site and encouraged people to witness the one day of the year when the rising sun lines up the Hele Stone, the Slaughter Stone, and the English Heritage souvenir shop. Every effort is being made to recreate Bronze Age Britain, including putting out traffic cones to block off the A344 at its junction with the A303, which archaeologists believe was how it must have looked back in 2000 B.C.

These days Stonehenge is a massively popular tourist attraction with more visitors than the site can cope with. Which is ironic really, because when it was built between 3000 and 1700 B.C. it was ruthlessly criticised as a Neolithic public relations disaster and a waste of Bronze Age lottery money. Many of the primitive Beaker people who inhabited England at the time felt that the money could have been much better spent on other things, such as beakers and well, er—more beakers.

For Stonehenge was, of course, the original Millennium Dome.* The rulers of ancient Britain decided that to celebrate a certain date on the calendar they should construct a huge circular monument that would be a source of great national pride and inspiration. Visitors would come from miles around and see real bodies being sacrificed in the Body Zone. They would understand the working of the sun and the stars in the Learning Zone. There was probably even an Environment Zone, although I'm sure no mention was ever made of how they managed to get planning permission to erect sixty-four-ton stones in the middle of Salisbury Plain.

But then things started to go wrong for the Stonehenge Experience Consortium. High-flying druids were delayed by security on the opening night. The projected twenty million visitors failed to materialise, unsurprising when the population of Britain was only a few thousand. "Fifty-seven bronze ingots for a family ticket!" exclaimed the local peasantry. "And that doesn't include having to buy eggs, chips, and mammoth at the Country Diner on the way down." And all this after it had taken more than a thousand years to complete. Archaeologists are divided as to whether this was due to shifting religious and cultural pressures or simply because the builders kept disappearing to work on another job. "Sorry mate, we're still waiting for those bloody rocks to be delivered from the Preseli Mountains. Of course we could have fin-

---

*The Dome was the British government's big idea for the new millennium. The idea was a sort of spiritual World's Fair but it came out more like Grand Central Station during the rush hour and it could be another 1,000 years before the government's PR department gets over it. My favourite national monument was Dublin's 120-metre-tall spire, which was erected to celebrate the forthcoming millennium. It was completed in March 2003.

ished it last week if you'd let us use a concrete lintel from Home Depot, but if you will insist on having traditional bluestone . . ."

Thousands of years have now passed and Stonehenge has now completely recovered from its shaky start and is now an enormously popular attraction. But its modern-day equivalent will not have five millennia to prove itself. This week it is halfway through its short life and now has no chance of meeting the original estimates for visitor numbers. To appease the modern-day gods of corporate sponsorship, various managing directors have already been dragged to the slaughter stone and publicly sacrificed. Before long Greenwich will become a mysterious historical site where archaeologists will debate the cultural significance of the building that once stood there. Was it a temple? A solar calculator? Or a sort of educational and cultural theme park thingy?

You don't need to go through the learning zone to understand that the Dome was tainted from the outset by politics. Everyone who dislikes this government was determined to hate the Dome with or without ever going there. And just as you could gauge the movements of the sun and the stars at Stonehenge, you could measure the waxing and waning of the government's popularity by reaction to the Millennium Dome.

The trouble was that everyone knew that the government really wanted you to go there. Nothing could be worse for attendance figures. For years Stonehenge was officially out of bounds and people were desperate to get in. Now the razor wire fences have been taken away from Salisbury Plain and access is permitted. But they should hang on to that fencing and put it up around the Dome. Tony Blair should go on record saying that we cannot have members of the public wandering all over this historical site—in fact, the government should make it illegal to trespass on the Millennium Dome. Attendance figures would double overnight.

MISSILE IMPOSSIBLE, PART TWO

12 July 2000

I t has been a difficult few days for Lieutenant General Ronald Kadish, director of America's Ballistic Missile Defense Organization. Over the weekend he invited a load of friends by to show them his new Intercontinental Missile Defence Shield, and isn't it always the way: the bloody thing didn't work. A Minuteman II was fired from Southern California. Another missile was fired from 4,500 miles away in the middle of the Pacific Ocean to intercept the oncoming warhead, but apparently the necessary electronic signal was not received at the correct time or something. That'll teach him not to read the manual beforehand.

It all happened so quickly: suddenly the missile was careering off target, billions of dollars of military hardware was heading in the wrong direction at 16,000 mph, and Ronald was frantically skimming through the chapter entitled "Care of your Minuteman Missile System." Then his wife had a better idea: "Quick, phone the helpline!" And while the president was demanding to know what was going on, the poor general was stuck listening to a recorded message that said, "Thank you for calling the ICBM helpline. If you wish to purchase other Minuteman missile systems, press 1. If you are phoning about our interest-free monthly payment plan, press 2. If your Intercontinental

Missile has malfunctioned and is hurtling toward Southern California, press 3 and hold for an operator." And then they played a tinny version of *Bolero* as the general watched $100 billion going up in smoke.

It was the most expensive fireworks display of all time, but though they all went "ooohhh" there was no "aaahhh." Not even Mrs. Kadish's delicious potato salad and the packet of sparklers could offer much consolation. Hundreds of people covered their eyes in embarrassed disbelief. It was like the premiere of John Travolta's *Battlefield Earth* all over again.

This is not the first time America's missile systems have missed their target. During the Gulf War, a great deal was made of the Patriot missiles' ability to knock out the oncoming Scuds. The Patriots were declared a huge success because out of twenty-two Scuds fired, twenty-one were intercepted. But this is where the U.S. military uses a different language from the rest of us, because as everyone remembers, lots of Scuds got through and caused enormous damage. So a Pentagon spokesman was eventually forced to explain (as if we were all really slow and stupid) that when they said "intercepted" they meant that the path of the Patriot crossed the path of the Scud, *though not necessarily at the same time*. So "intercepted" means "missed." He was later heard on the phone saying, "Darling I'm going to be home late tonight because I've intercepted my train."

If modern defence strategists had planned the D-day landings, the Allied forces would have found themselves wading ashore at Coney Island. Despite the United States spending $122 billion on missile defence systems, they have yet to develop anything that actually defends anyone against missiles. Perhaps I'm being overly picky, but you would have thought that this wasn't really good enough. And even though it is no longer clear who is going to declare war on the world's only superpower, the man who may well be the next president, George W. Bush, remains a great supporter of the "Star Wars" project. America may have token enemies like Iraq or Libya but they're no more likely to launch intercontinental missile attacks than Darth Vader himself. Instead of spending these unfeasibly large amounts of money on the unworkable National Defense Shield the Pentagon might as well buy a Super Soaker XP 2000 (slogan, "Wetter is Better"). Admittedly it is unlikely that this water pistol would actually intercept any incoming nuclear missiles, but it's got about the same chance as anything else they've tried so far, while having the advantage of being considerably cheaper. Even if the Pentagon eventually upgraded to the more expensive Super Soaker Monster XL with multiple nozzles and an extra large reservoir, they'd still save a fortune.

But of course, when it comes to military spending the cash is always available. The Pentagon could launch an aircraft carrier that didn't float and they'd still get the funding to build another one. Why is it that enormous amounts of taxpayers' money are always available for defence spending, and yet if it is education or health we always have to help make up the shortfall ourselves? You don't get soldiers' wives organising summer fetes to raise money for much-needed nuclear warheads. "Tank rides round the square, 50p." "Throw a wet sponge at the general—three goes for a pound." I suppose the sponge would only fly off in the wrong direction and land on the napalm barbecue. If the smart bombs were that smart they would decommission themselves and redirect the much-needed funding toward health, education, and overseas aid. Because it wasn't the missile that missed the real target this week. It was all that money that went up in smoke with it.

AFGHAN HOUNDS WELCOME; AFGHAN PEOPLE JOIN THE BACK OF THE LINE

9 July 2000

Yesterday Britain's first pet passports came into effect. Around the country dogs have been hopping into photo booths and trying to look as relaxed as possible, which is not easy when you know you are not allowed on the chair. In Britain's airports, dogs have been boarding planes bound for Europe, one item of mouth luggage only, and have then spent the entire flight staring at the passenger next to them with a look that says "I'll have your biscuit if you don't want it." Thirty thousand feet up, dog owners have been asking the stewardesses, "Can we open the window? He always likes to put his head out of the window. . . ."

Animals have had to wait more than a hundred years to get their own passports, which is only slightly longer than a lot of people have had to wait recently. Not one voice seems to have been raised in objection; not even the most ardent anti-immigrationists have accused this government about being "soft on rabies." *La rage* used to be this terrible plague that would sweep across Britain as soon as the first rat came through the channel tunnel. Ministers would warn that if the disease came to Britain, all of England's foxes would have to be shot. "Shame!" shouted the backbenchers, thinking of how that would deprive them of all the fun of ripping foxes to pieces with packs of dogs.

Quarantine conditions were so harsh and so expensive that every year hundreds of pets were smuggled into the country secretly hidden away inside large consignments of cocaine and heroin. Every summer British children suffered dislocated arms as nervous parents yanked them away from patting harmless poodles in the French countryside. It was all nonsense of course; nobody on the Continent gave a second thought to rabies. Anyway, racehorses were always exempt from the laws and could come and go into the United Kingdom as they pleased, unless of course they broke their leg in the Grand National, in which case they were fed to all the dogs in quarantine.

Now at last we have got over our irrational fear of rabies and all mammals can pass through customs without fear of being caged for six months. All mammals except asylum seekers, that is. So that's why they are abolishing quarantine for pets; they need all the cages for refugees. Afghan hounds are welcome; Afghan people get a bone and a bowl of water and are told to sit and stay.

What is it about the English that makes us love animals and dislike foreigners in almost equal measure? Why is it that the transport of veal calves in tiny crates prompts open weeping from demonstrators, and yet when the victims of political oppression are packed into prison ships it is described as luxurious first-class accommodation paid for by Britain's taxpayers? (It's a shame none of the asylum seekers ever murdered thousands of political opponents in Chile, or we could have put them up in a luxury mansion in Surrey.)*

---

*Former Chilean dictator General Pinochet was at that time being detained in great luxury by the British Government. They were going to make him secretary of state but they decided he was a bit soft on law and order.

The fear that we used to have of rabies was out of all proportion to the reality of the problem. The same is now true of asylum seekers. There is a madness that has swept Britain, but you don't get it from a dog bite, you get it from listening to politicians debating refugees. Britain is not suffering a terrible wave of immigration from bogus applicants who are sneaking past unnoticed while customs officers are patting all the Labradors now coming through the barrier. We currently take fewer refugees per capita than most countries in Western Europe; the idea that Britain is "soft on asylum seekers" is not only incorrect, but it is also a nauseating response to the wrong question. The issue should be why we are not doing more to help those who have been the victims of oppression. It seems that we don't mind dropping bombs on the Balkans, but ask us to pay £3 more council tax to help the refugees from that corner of Europe and the tabloids splash it across the front page as if this was the end of civilisation as we know it.

This week our siegelike island mentality took a very small step in the right direction: we have stopped being paranoid and have opened up our borders to pets. Everyone seems very relaxed about this; not even our leading politicians are concerned about rabies. But this is because since immigration returned to the political agenda, they're foaming at the mouth already.

NEW BALLS, PLEASE

19 July 2000

This week English sports fans witnessed a sight even grimmer than the plaid trousers worn by the golfers at the U.S. Open. England's Davis Cup team lost to Ecuador, a country whose tennis facilities are so limited that their training schedule was relegated to playing Swingball in the coach's back garden. You could tell they'd been underfunded because every time the ball boys threw them another tennis ball they got out a marker pen and scrawled their initials on it.

This latest sporting humiliation comes after the England soccer team's dismal showing in Euro 2000 and years of failure in cricket, rugby, and just about every sport that has ever been devised. British golfers consistently come in a poor second and then blame the American golf courses for their lack of little windmills and helter-skelters. The rally-cross team spent four hours on a lay-by arguing with Triple A about their expired membership. The UK's Olympic orienteering team couldn't find the stadium. The ladies' swimming champion kept tutting because the German in the next lane was splashing too much and wetting her hair. When it comes to picking the world's great sporting nations, Britain is the fat kid with asthma left standing against the wall.

There are all sorts of reasons why my country underachieves on the sports field. If you read the right-wing papers you will discover that it's all down to those politically correct left-wing authorities who banned competitive sport and forced our most promising athletes to channel their energies into lesbian peace workshops. But obviously it is in fact all the fault of the Conservatives who presided over the selling off of school playing fields, underinvestment in education, and a failure to provide the sort of training facilities that are available in more successful sporting countries like, er, Ecuador.

Perhaps there is something in the English national character that makes us not want to appear too pushy. When two British soccer players are going for the same ball, is there a nagging doubt at the back of their minds that they ought to be saying "Oh, I'm so sorry," "No, no, after you . . ." National sportsmen and women are supposed to provide us with role models—to reflect Britain's international status and importance in the world. And in consistently underachieving and disappointing us they have been doing a fantastic job. What foreign athletes fail to understand is that it is not winning, but losing dismally that counts.

When I was at school, the people like myself who were not very good at sport adopted a sneering contempt for anything vaguely athletic, so that we could pretend it was simply all far beneath us. This is the only way for England to salvage any dignity from the next World Cup. The English players should hang around behind the changing rooms smoking, spitting, and occasionally flicking their ties at all the better players as they turn up.

"Oi Ronaldo, you goody-goody! You don't actually *like* games, do you? Ugh—look, he's putting shorts on, the big nancy."

Then when the referee demands that the English players get changed, they can wave a tatty forged note from their mum under his nose and claim, "I'm excused from games, I've got a verucca."

Some of Britain's most revered sportsmen already behave like this; I remember seeing one of our leading soccer players staggering around with a can of lager in one hand and a kebab in the other. I wasn't surprised when he was taken off at halftime.

There was of course a brief period in history when Britain was unbeatable on the playing field, but we achieved this with the rather crafty trick of inventing all the sports ourselves to give us a head start. This has to be the way forward once again. We should examine what it is we are good at, develop these pastimes into fully fledged sports, and then dominate them for a few decades. For example it's all very well throwing a shot put a long way, but no one can throw the plastic chair from a Belgian café as far as an England soccer fan. Soon we will hear the sports anchor promising a great evening of sporting action: "Tonight on the BBC, highlights of last night's thrilling clash between the Belgian water cannon and Fat Degsy from Manchester. We have a chance to see Britain's gold medal hopefuls in the synchronised rioting and then it's over to court number one for the Police versus Innocent Deported Soccer Fan."

All these new events will be organised into a special international tournament at which Britain can showcase the sports that will dominate the new century. It is our chance to be first once more. Except we all know what will happen, of course—at the last moment our bid to host the games will be beaten by bloody Ecuador.

57 CHANNELS AND NOTHING ON

10 August 2000

I saw a newspaper headline recently that proclaimed "THE DIGITAL DECEPTION—Most Viewers Won't Notice the Difference, Says TV Watchdog." If only this were true. The depressing thing is that when we do all have 200 television channels we really will notice the difference. There won't be anything to watch.*

Why do the people who bring us all this extra "choice" presume that more is necessarily better? Are they suggesting that there is so much great TV on the existing terrestrial channels that there just isn't room for it all? "Coming up on ITV2—all the outtakes from *Central Heating Engineers from Hell* that we couldn't show on ITV1 because there just wasn't time." New technology is a wonderful thing, but just because we *can* do something doesn't mean we *should* do something. We have the ability to travel to the moon but realized pretty quickly that if we want to go to a lifeless desert we can go for a weekend minibreak in Belgium.

Difficult though it must be for an American to imagine, for most of our lives us Brits have had only three or four television channels to choose from, or less at Buckingham Palace, where they have yet to discover the button for commerical television.

Apparently one of the great advantages of digital TV is that it is interactive. At last—I can choose from which camera I watch a televised football game. Obviously that is infinitely preferable to having a professional sports director make these decisions for me. Then we are told that the quality of the sound and picture is superior on digital TV. Isn't that rather missing the point? Fantastic! A clearer sound on *The Jerry Springer Show*. Wouldn't it be better if we *couldn't* hear what that obese woman from West Virginia was shouting at her husband's mistress, who is also his transsexual sister?

It's not the quality of the reception on my TV set that depresses me late at night when I am too tired to get off the sofa and I flick through all those endless free channels until my head aches and frustration eventually drives me upstairs to bed. It's like tasting your way through two dozen different cups of noodles in search of a satisfying meal. One channel I had thought worth watching had originally featured old black-and-white films, which were the perfect late-night viewing. That obviously can't have made them any money because now a glance at the TV listings tells me that this week's highlights include such artistic triumphs as *Scary Sex*, *Erotic Confessions*, and *Can You Keep It Up for a Week*. This is the dismal fate of so many channels that are struggling to hold onto even the tiniest audience share (and incidentally, the denouement of *Erotic Confessions* was all over the place).

Another brilliantly pointless idea is twenty-four-hour news channels. It's 4 A.M. and you want to know how the election campaign for the Scottish parliament is going: you just switch to channel 49 and they will keep you bang up to date on all the developments since 3 A.M. The Scottish secretary will be sitting there in his pajamas being grilled by the sad newsreader who's available at this hour only because his wife left him.

"Minister—will the government's strategy be changing in response to the fact that the Scottish electorate appear to have gone to bed?"

"Er, no—this is perfectly normal at this stage in the campaign—there's nothing to say, why did you wake me up?"

"Hang on, we have to interrupt you there, Minister, because we have some breaking news—Prime Minister Tony Blair has just rolled over in his sleep and mumbled 'I wish those Serbian demonstrators outside Downing Street would shut up!'—more on that and other stories at 5 A.M."

Other new channels on the way include Climate Classics, featuring those golden weather reports from the 1960s and '70s, and the Home Shoplifting Channel, where you see something you like on the Shopping Channel and then they go round and nick it for you. Not one of these channels is honest enough to call itself The Rubbish Channel—because that is what you get when you try to make TV programs for nothing. Yet more and more new low-budget television stations keep appearing until eventually the remote control will be larger than the TV set, it will have two hundred buttons, and the only one that we'll need will be the button that says "Off."

HOARDING THE
COUNTRYSIDE

30 August 2000

Wordsworth's famous lines will soon need to be updated. "I wandered lonely as a cloud / That floats on high o'er vale and hill, / When all at once I saw a huge billboard telling me about Taco Bell's chalupas." The government has announced that advertising hoardings will now be permitted across most of the English countryside. Clearly the millions of visitors to our shores this summer were disappointed that the views across rural England were not obscured by enormous posters and so the government has stepped in to put this right. We are assured that we will still see beautiful scenery in rural England, but only as featured on the poster advertising the new Volkswagen.

Now the chitchat in the English countryside will be changed forever. "Ooh, I've got terrible problems; no rain for a month, winter cabbage gone to seed, and the focus group has revealed that the branding concept on my poster sites is failing to reach the targeted age groups." Once farmers have got the advertising bug they might find other ways to get the message across. The sheep won't just be herded into a pen; the collies will have to arrange them on the hillside to spell out "It's always Coca-Cola." Bright yellow mustard will be planted in such a formation that airline passengers flying over-head will see the Nike logo. Bored-looking cows will stand around in fields holding placards that say "Men's Clothing Sale—left at the corner."

There are always more places in which commercials can be placed. Soon it won't be possible to have a hearing aid fitted that doesn't contain a tape that privately plays you the Jolly Green Giant jingle every five minutes. Or what about advertising during the Queen's Christmas message to her subjects? "At this festive time one's thoughts turn to the Commonwealth, but also to the fact that the World of Leather sale starts at 9 A.M. at your local mall."

The trouble is of course that the more advertisements to which we are exposed, the less effective they become. The first piece of junk mail was probably read quite carefully. The government giving per-mission to increase the number of poster sites won't result in a corre-sponding rise in consumption of all the products advertised. We are still going to buy only one car each, Elton John excepted. Advertis-ing might persuade us to switch from Coca-Cola to Pepsi but it won't make us spend money we haven't got on things we don't want.

The proliferation of advertising is steadily eating away our qual-ity of life and is becoming increasingly ineffective as it does so. And the idea that the financial crisis facing British farming can be solved with roadside posters is clearly ridiculous. The farmers in greatest need live in the remotest areas and have no sites of any value. It is true that the more accessible areas of rural England do receive thousands of visitors every year but it is precisely because they are unspoilt. The act of erecting poster sites will in itself help make the sites valueless. Somehow I can't imagine myself driving down to Somerset to look at the view of Michael Jordan eating a Nathan's hot dog.

The way forward is to combine two problems to create an overall solution. While it is banning fox hunting the government should add an amendment legalising the hunting of advertising executives. Yuppie account handlers will be strolling around the countryside checking out their new advertising hoardings when suddenly the horn will sound and packs of hounds will descend upon them, snapping at their Armani suits as red-coated huntsmen gallop across the fields in pursuit. It will become one of the beautiful traditional sights of the English countryside. It's a shame that the billboards will prevent anyone from actually seeing it.

N.B. *The British government later reversed its policy on this issue, but were only just dissuaded from putting posters up all over the Yorkshire dales to advertise the fact.*

OWN GOAL

13 September 2000

Tony Blair and Gerhard Schroeder had high-level talks about the problem of football transfers last week. This was, of course, the official spin to cover up the embarrassing outburst that always happens when English people start arguing with the Germans about soccer; namely that Tony Blair drank too much lager and stood on the table singing "Two world wars and one World Cup, doo-dah, doo-dah!"

These days every British politician finds it expedient to have an interest in the beautiful game. Soon the leader of the opposition will be claiming he's always loved soccer ball, and since he was a lad he's supported the Liverpool Dolphins. And just to show that he's still in touch and is concerned about standards, he'll suggest the introduction of league tables for soccer clubs.

The latest story to concern our politicians is the impending abolition of transfer fees, which threatens to have very serious consequences for Britain's smaller clubs. This issue is like those maps of flooded Britain after the polar ice cap has melted. Your eye goes straight to the bit where you live; you see that your house will still be on dry land and then you stop worrying about it.

The issue is that the system by which players are transferred from one club to another is apparently in breach of European employment law. We are told that workers are not sold from one company to the next in any other area of commerce; you don't get labourers being sold from one building firm to another, say the critics. But of course, footballers are not like builders. I have never seen David Beckham beat three defenders and then suddenly leave the ball in the middle of the goalmouth to go and play in another game over on the other side of town.

Soccer is more than just a business in which brands are competing in the marketplace. You don't get thousands of Pepsi and Coke drinkers chanting abuse at each other: "You've got no teeth anymoooore!" Fathers don't say to their sons, "I'm taking you to Woolworth's on Saturday, son, because this family has shopped at Woolworth's for three generations."

Maybe the way forward is not for soccer to become more like other businesses, but for the world of commerce and politics to become more like soccer. Important economic and political issues should not be settled by politicians voting or shareholders' meetings but by penalty shoot-outs. At last the issue of European monetary union would get the attention it deserves. "And you join us here at Le Stade de France at a crucial moment in our economic history where Britain's adoption of the European currency is about to be decided on penalties. The very existence of the English pound now depends on the goalkeeping skills of young Tony Blair as Jacques Chirac bravely steps onto the spot for the first kick. . . ."

And like the French and Italian coaches working in Britain, Blair should be able to sign the best politicians from Europe and the rest of the world. Then the political commentators could stand outside Downing Street in a sheepskin coat with a couple of young fans waving at the camera in the background as they bring us exciting news of the latest signing: "Joining the cabinet this week, Blair's record £5 million signing from the French government, Lionel Jospin, who'll be making his debut today as Minister for Defence." English front-bench politicians who have failed to make their mark in the top flight over here could be sold to foreign parliaments and would find their natural level by joining the opposition in Cyprus or Slovakia.

Perhaps these were the changes discussed last week by Tony Blair and Gerhard Schroeder. But somehow you get the feeling that whenever politicians kick around the subject of soccer it's in the hope that some of the popularity of the world's most popular sport will rub off on them. Any way that you look at the figures, more people tune into the World Cup final than the debates on the Parliament Channel.

So maybe it's for the best that the cultures of politics and football do not grow any closer. Otherwise we might get to a situation where politicians were only motivated by money, where winning was all that mattered, and where members of the House of Commons started to behave like some sort of unruly rabble, jeering and shouting abuse at supporters of the other side. And that would be too awful to imagine.

VOUS ÊTES DANS L'ARMÉE, MAINTENANT

11 October 2000

This week it was proposed that the Royal Air Force would soon be engaging with the German armed services. Margaret Thatcher must have thought it the best birthday present she could have wished for, until someone explained, "No, Margaret, we mean British and German forces *on the same side.*"

The idea of a European Rapid Reaction Force has been gaining ground ever since the debacle of Kosovo, even though the words "European" and "rapid" do not normally sit that comfortably together. The reasoning is that with the Americans becoming less willing to finance military interventions, the European Union should have its own defence capability based in Brussels, to operate independently of NATO, which is based in, er, Brussels. Then European military powers like Britain and France could combine to launch operations without having to seek the approval of the United States. Well it worked so well in Suez, so why not?

It is claimed that language would not be a problem—apparently European soldiers would find the upper-class British officer just as incomprehensible as English soldiers always have done. But it's hard to imagine that in the heat of battle the odd second might not be lost. A British corporal would shout "Enemy fire! Take cover!" and then all the continental troops would get out their Petit Larousse English/French dictionaries and eventually smile and reply, "Yes, I am liking the Beatles also."

The British government is actually one of the leading advocates of the so-called European Defence Identity, although if it came to any major conflict the outbreak of war would then be delayed while each of fifteen member states organised a referendum. The establishment of a European Defence Identity would at least bring military decisions back to the countries deploying the troops, but because the European Union does not have a single president or prime minister, any military intervention would have to be agreed to by committee. Why on earth would fifteen different European heads of state want to use military force at once—they can't all have elections coming up at the same time.

With the planned expansion of the European Union to eventually include Turkey, Chad, and Australia, it's hard to know against whom the EU could launch an attack. If I were a soldier in Switzerland I would be getting very nervous around now, especially since the Swiss Army has only those little penknives with which to defend themselves.

"Er, Sarge, do any of these blades fold out into an antitank missile grenade launcher?"

"Um, I don't think so—but there's a little pair of nail scissors there, you could really hurt someone with that."

The deeper problem of course is not how to organise military intervention but whether it generally works or not. The people of Serbia did not overthrow Slobodan Milosevic because NATO dropped bombs on them a few months back. And if NATO was sincere in its claim that it bombed Belgrade for humanitarian reasons, let's now see the same countries spend more on helping rebuild Serbia than they spent on the bombs that helped destroy it.

Any new force will soon learn that military action is always easier to embark on than it is to curtail. Throughout history political leaders have gone to war and found themselves in a longer conflict than they had expected. When poor Edward III got embroiled in the Hundred Years' War he said, "Blimey, I didn't think it was going to go on this long," and his advisors said, "Well, the actual name of your war might have raised the odd suspicion, Your Majesty."

If there's to be a European rapid reaction force, then its use must be limited to emergency and humanitarian aid. They could try developing a full-blown European army but there'd be only one outcome. As the various units sought to wield military power without clear political leadership, arguments would break out among the various European ethnic groups. Minor skirmishes between British, French, and German troops would escalate, nation-states would mobilise, and Europe would once more be plunged into all-out war. Still, I suppose it would save us having to make a decision on monetary union for another few years.

A MAN IS ROBBED EVERY TWENTY MINUTES* (*AND HE'S GETTING PRETTY FED UP WITH IT)

18 October 2000

Politicians from all sides have been discussing the new crime figures this week and the statistics make depressing reading. When talking about action against burglars, use of the word "tough" has increased 57 percent. But when referring to violent crime, incidents of politicians saying "tough" has gone up by a massive 71 percent. We are more likely to be assaulted by the phrase "more policemen on the beat" than at any time in the past twenty years, and millions now live in fear of the trauma of waking up to discover that the Home Secretary is talking on the radio news.

Meanwhile the British Crime Survey has actually revealed that crime itself is going down. There are fewer burglaries, except in the areas where people keep going out and leaving the house to attend Neighbourhood Watch meetings. There is a reduction in motor vehicle crime, which is attributed to car alarms, while the increase in parked cars being attacked with a sledgehammer in the middle of the night is also attributed to car alarms. Apparently we are more likely to be robbed and assaulted by strangers, but this is hardly surprising— if you're going to mug someone you'd have to be pretty stupid to try it out on your best friend.

Although the figures are falling, a huge percentage of crime continues to be committed by young males. There is a simple way of rectifying this imbalance: the government should introduce lots of new offences for everyone else. All sorts of antisocial behaviour continues to go unchecked in our society. For example, if you are in a long line it should be unlawful for the person right in front of you to suddenly be joined by lots of friends. It's no good, them just thinking up something completely inconsequential to say about having parked the car, just to show you that they know each other. Then if you arrive in the cinema after the film has started, it should be an offence not to duck slightly as you walk across the front. If the film ends five minutes before last orders it should also be against the law to sit there in deep contemplation, waiting to see who was "Key Grip" while everyone else on your row has stood up and is desperate to get out and grab a swift beer.

Leaving the scene of a jammed photocopier should be a criminal offence. And there should also be a new offence of corporate stalking. I have been stalked by the telephone company for several years now. They keep ringing me up when I least expect it, saying they know who I called last month and trying to force me to buy discounted rates to Brazil.

Of course it could be argued that we don't need any new offences when there are so many crimes that are ignored already. None of the reporting on this week's crime figures made any reference to city fraud or big business tax evasion. Where are the interviews with old ladies saying how they are afraid to go out lest they should be offered a tip for some insider trading? Where are the big yellow signs in the City of London saying "Appeal for Witnesses—Fraud. Did you see any-one skimming the remainders fund, selling currency forward, and then buying it spot-fixed overnight? And more to the point, can you ex-plain what this means?"

There are all sorts of reasons why crime has fallen and many voters will be alienated by anyone trying to score party political points on this issue. But before the election Tony Blair promised to be "Tough on Crime and Tough on the Causes of Crime" and the latest crime figures suggest his approach may be working. Okay, so he nicked the phrase off one of his ministers. But you can't blame Labour for that; the Conservatives were in power when it happened.

BRITAIN LASHED
BY HURRICANE!

1 November 2000

F ew people in Britain will forget the extreme conditions they experienced this week. For hour after hour they were battered with relentless press coverage of the storm, clichés rained down as tabloid readers were forced to wade through pages and pages of storm supplement extras. Brave commuters battled through anecdotes about their journey into work, sometimes taking several hours and often involving huge diversions to recount how they managed back in the hurricane of 1987. Power lines were down in some areas, though not enough to stop millions having to endure Trevor MacDonald's "Storm and Travel Special." Though the travel report on the radio was actually shorter than normal. It just said "Travel news now—and you can't travel anywhere."

Journalists have a special computer programme for this sort of news event called Microsoft Hack-writer. You just type in the word "weather" and then you're presented with the options "Hot," "Wet," or "Cold" and the story just writes itself. There were one or two early editions in Britain yesterday where journalists using Microsoft Hack had clearly experienced one or two software problems: "In the wettest October day since records began, tarmac melted from the heat

as sheep were rescued from snowdrifts and whole reservoirs dried up
bringing volunteers to airlift fish to safety from the rising floodwaters."

The only thing that any visitor to Britain needs to understand
about a crisis like the one we experienced this week is that *we just
love it*. A drama that involved everyone rallying around, making cups
of tea, rescuing animals, and talking about the weather to boot; the
British were in pure heaven on Monday. "It was just like the blitz,"
said one commentator, although this time if people spent all night
in the underground, it would have been because their trains were
stuck in the tunnel as usual for twelve hours. The railways did remarkably well in that the service was barely changed from the one
they'd provided in the week before the storm. There was the same
excuse for cancellations that we get every autumn, although to be
fair this year the leaves on the track still had the rest of the trees
attached to them. Ferries were unable to dock at the channel ports,
causing serious shortages of smuggled cigarettes. The damage to property ran into millions of pounds, which means that the insurance
companies may end up having to pay out anything up to £17.50.

Labour ministers might try pointing out that though the experience of Monday's storm was distressing, the hurricane that Britain
suffered under Mrs. Thatcher's government was in fact a lot worse.
But of course there is a real political point to be made. There have
been floods all over the world in the past few years. Four thousand
people killed in China, thousands made homeless by mudslides in
Venezuela, devastating floods in the Italian Alps and western United
States; these events put a few ruined carpets in Cornwall into some
sort of perspective. But now there's another storm on the horizon.
The People's Fuel Lobby is planning to bring the country to a halt
all over again in its campaign to reduce the tax on gasoline. Never
mind that gasoline consumption is considered a major factor in the
world's climate changes, never mind that half the country will be per-

manently underwater in fifty years' time; as long as it doesn't cost too much to get out the Land Rover Discovery and run Hermione to her gymkhana, that's the main thing. So that's why so many Conservatives own those huge 4 x 4s. Okay, so they may use up more gasoline but that doesn't matter because when the ice cap does melt, the status symbol jeep is just that bit better at getting through the flood water. I suppose that's why they all have little bolt-holes in the hills as well—when London is finally completely underwater, they can just escape to the cottage in Gloucestershire until the government sorts it all out.

After the burning of fossil fuels, our second greatest source of greenhouse gases is apparently from the methane from cows' bottoms. But with the amount of bullshit coming from the fuel protestors at the moment this figure looks set to rise as well. I just wish that they had held their protest on Monday; it would have been fun to watch them out in the storm trying to bring the country to a standstill as hurricanes and floods completely upstaged them. Yes, there is a problem with gasoline prices. They are just not high enough. Either we stop using our cars so much, or the permanent flooding of half of the country will mean that we stop using them altogether. They used to give out free glasses with gasoline. They should start giving out sandbags and life jackets instead.

THE 43RD PRESIDENT OF THE UNITED STATES IS—ER . . .

15 November 2000

I cried on the day President Kennedy was shot. I was lying in my cot and I'd dropped my pacifier through the bars. Next week sees the anniversary of that infamous assassination, and America looks set to commemorate it by killing off another rightful president. For years the debate will rage—was the Florida judge acting alone or was it part of some wider conspiracy? Was there a second judge hiding behind the grassy knoll? Show that film again—there's definitely a second hole going into that ballot paper.

There is of course a difference between Kennedy and Gore. Kennedy won the presidency by only 100,000 votes, whereas Gore beat Bush by more than twice that. We are often told that America is the greatest democracy in the world. Well, yes, apart from the minor quibbles that less than half of the electorate voted and the bloke who got fewer votes looks set to win. Soon the billions spent on the election will be as nothing compared to all the BBC journalists' hotel bills for their extended stays in Washington. "It could never happen in Britain, of course," they all say smugly. Except it has happened in Britain twice since the war, most spectacularly in 1951, when the Labour government got the highest percentage poll of any political party since the advent of universal suffrage and was still thrown out of office. And who can forget the things that Winston Churchill's 1951–55 government then did without a proper mandate? Well, we all can, as it turns out, but that's not the point. Britain can hardly feel smug about its own democratic safeguards when its own head of state was chosen by dint of being the eldest daughter of an accidentally crowned king, descended from a foreign prince who was brought in at the last minute to keep out the Catholics. (I don't see why the Conservatives are so paranoid about England being ruled by the Germans, when they've been sitting on the British throne since George I.)

The difference in this case of course is that events in Florida will affect the whole world. Live coverage is being beamed to London, Paris, and Moscow, while in Chad, the president is saying loudly, "It's also the name of an African country, you know, not just a little bit of paper."

Immediately as it became apparent that neither presidential candidate had won decisively, all sorts of accusations and recriminations started being thrown about. Gore was told he blew it by not being enough like Clinton. Instead of going around shaking people's hands he should have locked himself in the stationery cupboard with an intern. Then it was claimed that some ballot papers were so confusing that less intelligent electors voted for the wrong person. So at least Al Gore got Dubya's vote. Meanwhile careful analysis of the figures show that the governor of Texas has been seeking to gain an unfair advantage over the past few years by executing more Democrats than Republicans. It must be said that as political dynasties go, they don't come much less glamorous than the Bush family. If the original President Bush had been made into a film, would anyone have bothered with a sequel? But now in the land where anyone is supposed to be able to reach the White House, the son of the last Republican president looks set to inherit it because of dubious electoral practices in the state where his brother is governor. So that's why George W. Bush went into politics. He wanted to spend more time with his family.

There must be a simple way to sort this all out. Can't we have a special TV quiz to ask both candidates a few general knowledge questions such as "Where is Africa?" Then the host could say "George W.—you are the weakest link—good-bye!" Or maybe a more American way would be for the two candidates to fight it out in the style of the World Wrestling Federation: Al "The Jogger" Gore versus George "The Executioner" Bush. It would still look less fixed than the result in Florida.

Of course if Gore does end up losing the presidency, he could still have a brief taste of the top job. If I were Bill Clinton I'd resign the day before Bush is inaugurated, just to give his deputy a whole twenty-four hours as president. This would just be enough time for Bill to take him round the Oval Office and show him the ropes. "Al, here's your desk, look—I had them make up a little nameplate saying 'Al Gore, President.' Take a seat, Al, how does it feel?" Then "President Gore" could sit down and open up his diary to see what his duties were for the day. "Let's see, Saturday, Saturday. . . . Ah yes, here we are: 4 P.M.—*hand over the presidency to George W. Bush.*" "Now I wouldn't sit there too long, Al, you might want to go and practice your dignified smile for George's inauguration ceremony."

If George W. Bush does succeed in stealing the presidency from under the noses of the American people it will be the most audacious political crime since Adolf Hitler poured gasoline through the letterbox of the Reichstag and still got the money from the insurance company. The only hope is that come inauguration day, George W. will trip over his words again and fail to be sworn in as president. Because some of his recent statements suggest he might not be quite up to the world's top job. "I was raised in the West. The west of Texas.

It's pretty close to California. In more ways than Washington, D.C., is close to California." He's even stronger on economics: "It's clearly a budget; it's got a lot of numbers in it." And on the environment: "Natural gas is hemispheric. I like to call it hemispheric in nature because it is a product that we can find in our neighbourhoods." I've had gym teachers smarter than George W. Bush. We knew that some American voters had an anti-intellectual streak but they didn't have to go that far. But as George famously said himself, "They misunderestimated me." When Dubya takes his seat in the Oval Office the global village will finally be complete. At last it will have its own global village idiot.

ONLY 16 SHOPLIFTING DAYS LEFT TILL CHRISTMAS

8 December 2000

When does the Christmas season officially begin? In the 1970s and '80s you knew the season of good will and joy to all mankind had arrived when the IRA started blowing up shopping centres. And we'd all tut and say, "Honestly, the IRA's Christmas bombing campaign starts earlier every year." But these days it's harder to know the exact moment when the festive season has really arrived. Is it the day the Christmas lights are switched on in the West End? Or is it the next day when they break down again and some poor bloke has to go all the way down Oxford Street checking every single bulb? For some people it is the delivery of the first charity catalogue, when the family gathers round excitedly to flick through this year's selection of raffia-work table mats. For others it is the first domestic argument about where they will be eating their roast turkey and chestnut stuffing. "I am not spending Christmas day at your brother's flat in Birmingham." "Well, we're certainly not having your father here again, not after last year with my sister. Mistletoe is not a license for tongues."

Of course moaning about Christmas starting too early is now part of the tradition itself. That's the wonderful thing about the festive season: the way it evolves and changes to incorporate new customs. And everything that now characterises a modern Christmas will one day seem as ancient a tradition as the Yule log and Nat King Cole singing "White Christmas." The new customs will be featured on Christmas cards of the future; just as today we send pictures of rosy-cheeked Dickensian children singing Christmas carols in the snow, cards in the next century will depict nostalgic scenes of drunken clerks in nylon Santa hats staggering out of office parties and being sick on the subway on the way home.

The tradition of sending Christmas cards has evolved into a complex and subtle form of communication. Although the message usually says something like "Season's Greetings," what this actually means varies according to the sender. Some cards say "I expect a Christmas tip"; others say "I'm still holding a candle for you," while one card I get every year says "You had Chinese delivered from our restaurant once and we made a note of your address." Then of course there is the mystery card. Somewhere in Britain there is a man with a very strange sense of humour who for years now has been sending cards to each and every one of us with the name of a made-up couple at the bottom. "Merry Christmas from Roy and Jane." "Who the bloody hell are Roy and Jane?" you say. "Was it that couple we met on holiday? No, it must be someone from your work. . . ." "Is that a 'Jane' or is it a 'James'? Do we know a gay couple called Roy and James?" and all the while the sender is chuckling to himself as he sends out another thousand cards from "Lesley and Colin," from "Alan and Miranda," and from "Piers and Nicola," knowing that everyone will be worrying about who it is that they have left off their Christmas card list. It must be even worse for the Royal Family; they get thousands of cards. Prince Philip must say, "We've got one from Edith Harris, 93 Station Road, Swansea." "Oh dear . . ." says the Queen. "I don't think we sent her one . . ."

The royals have a lot to answer for when it comes to Christmas traditions. Quite apart from the Queen's Christmas message, which is unfair, because ordinary people can't answer back, they are to blame for the practise of buying Christmas trees. Some people feel it is never really Christmas until they have driven across town with a twelve-foot tree sticking out of the side window knocking pensioners to the ground. The custom was of course introduced in the nineteenth century by Prince Albert. "I know!" said Victoria's husband excitedly. "Why don't we get everyone to use all those high school parking lots that are empty in the holidays to sell dead conifers to one another!" and the ministers looked at each other anxiously. "Yes," he went on, "then people can take these trees home and put them in the lounge for a few weeks until all the needles fall off and then they can be chucked into the front garden where they can stay for the whole year because the dustmen will refuse to take them!" And because Albert was a prince, no one had the nerve to tell him that this was a really stupid idea and so the convention survives to this day.

It was the royals of two thousand years ago who started the tradition of present giving as well. Those three kings (who of Orient were) gave the first-ever Christmas gifts to the newborn messiah. Of course if it was today he would have got a little bib with the slogan "I dribble for the Lakers" or a plastic Dinosaurs beaker from the Disney shop, but obviously it was early days for the Christmas gifts industry so he had to make do with some last-minute frankincense and myrrh from the nearby Bethlehem 7-11, while the gold was put in the junior savings account where Jesus couldn't touch it until he was twenty-one.

That was all two thousand years ago and the people who celebrate December 25 because it is Jesus' birthday have been waiting ever since for it to happen all over again. But they must realise that any chance of a second coming has been completely snuffed out. Because God must look down at the lametta and the spray-on snow, at the repeats of *Miracle on 34th Street* or David Bowie singing "The Little Drummer Boy," he must watch all the dads moaning because the kids have nicked the batteries from the TV remote control to put in their new laser guns, he must see all the unwanted junk that is bought and then thrown away; all the tension that builds from the middle of November until the depressing anticlimax of December 26 and all to the endless soundtrack of "Jingle Bells" and God must say to himself, "Second Coming? Nope, there's no way we're going to go through all that *twice* a year."

NATURE VERSUS NURTURE—
AWAY WIN

17 February 2001

This week a team of international scientists shared the incredible revelation that *Homo sapiens* has around 30,000 genes. There was then a pause while everyone tried to gauge whether they should be amazed that this number was so high or so low. It transpires that they'd been expecting the American citizens from which they took their samples to have many more genes than the nematode worm, but I suppose that's what happens when you base your research on the president. Worms were used in the genome project because it was presumed that their genetic code would be so simple to decipher that everyone could knock off early on Friday afternoon. But now the papers have had to report the uncomfortable truth that there's not that much difference between ourselves and the worm; the simple, primitive, stupid worm. Frankly worms have been patronised terribly in the media this week, and ought to take their case to the courts, except they won't of course, because they're so bloody stupid. Alongside the illustration of the humble nematode, all the papers featured similar drawings of a *Homo sapiens*—though the human in the tabloids had bigger breasts. The other creature that was analysed was the fruit fly. It turns out that these have around 13,000 genes, which sounds like more than they need. You'd have thought there were only two pieces of information you needed to give a fruit fly: (1) You fly. (2) You like fruit.

Whereas we humans, we're so clever, surely we must have millions and millions of genes? Not so, apparently; we have only five times more than yeast and the scientists tell us that we need only 11 percent of those. The rest are all junk apparently, although I would be reluctant to throw them out just yet.

The only conclusion that can be drawn from this is that if less information is genetically inherited, then more of our behaviour must be determined by social factors. There's nothing in the male's genetic makeup that instructs him to leave two bits of sweet corn at the bottom of the sink after he's washed up. There is no female gene that makes her want to have a taste of everyone else's pudding. Most of our behaviour is acquired. People who say that our behaviour is predetermined say that only because their mom and dad did.

The nature versus nurture question is as old as human society itself (unless it's even older and we inherited the debate from a bunch of precocious gorillas). But now the balance has shifted irreversibly in favour of those who believe that people are the same all over the world. The multimillion-dollar genome research project has reached the same conclusion as the lyrics of "Ebony and Ivory." It is of course a left versus right issue. Conservative politics are based on the philosophy that people just are the way they are, and that it's their own fault if they don't do more with their lives. George W. Bush is president because he worked harder and was more brilliant than some black woman who grew up in a one-parent family in Detroit—end of story. If you believe people are born good or bad or clever or stupid then there is no point in trying to change the world. The Australian penal colonies were founded on the belief that there was simply a criminal class who begat more criminals and if they could all be exported then crime would disappear from society. The idea got a huge cheer at the 1800 Conservative Party conference though it would probably be considered a bit liberal today. If it was true then modern-day Sydney would still be full of people stealing silk handkerchiefs and spending their money on cheap gin.

Irrespective of how many genes we have, the genome project has confirmed what many of us had instinctively known for a very long time: that nurture counts for more than nature. The debate is over forever; clearly the worm just wriggles around in mud all day because it just never got the breaks in life. But at a time when the fate of all the creatures on the planet depends on us, a little humility would not do mankind any harm, even if it's hard to accept that we have so much in common with such a basic life-form as yeast. After all, what has yeast ever done? It just reproduces in enormous numbers, consumes everything within its environment, and then finally poisons itself with the toxins it has produced. You could hardly imagine us humans ever doing anything so stupid.

ARTIFICIAL INTELLIGENCE IS OVER MY HEAD

3 March 2001

This week scientists claimed that after years of development and billions of dollars they had finally come up with a computer that could communicate with the linguistic skills of the average toddler. Which means that the computer just shouts "No!" at every reasonable suggestion you make and then throws itself to the floor of the supermarket while other shoppers look at you and tut.

"I know, PC, let's go to the swings after this!"

"I want Mommy!"

"Yes, well Mommy's just having a little sleep because you woke her up four times last night . . ."

"I want Mommy!"

And eventually you just stick another floppy disk in the A drive to keep it quiet even though you haven't actually paid for it yet.

Computers have come a very long way in a very short space of time. Apparently there is more digital technology in the average mobile phone than there was on the spacecraft that put the first man on the moon. Which is why Neil Armstrong didn't spend his whole time annoying his fellow astronauts by braying, "Ya, hi, I'm on a lunar module—ya, we're just arriving at the moon now . . ." So while

Apollo 11 may have looked impressive, there's no way it could have ever played an irritating electronic version of "The Entertainer." It's amazing the things computers can do today. You can change the number of tropical fish on your screen saver, you can have the flying toasters go fast or slow, you can play solitaire on-screen instead of with a pack of cards. How previous generations managed without such basic essentials is unimaginable. And following this week's break-through we are now promised microchips that will think and talk like real human beings. Cue a thousand crappy sci-fi films about computers taking over the world.

My PC already has its own personality—it is an unhelpful French bureaucrat: you try to reason with it but it just repeats the same thing back at you over and over again. I might try and get it reprogrammed so that when it refuses to cooperate, it does so in a French accent. "Zere eez no disk een drive A." "No, there is a disk, I just checked," and I attempt to back up my document again . . .

"Zere eez no disk een drive A."

"THERE IS A BLOODY DISK, LOOK, THERE IT IS! I'VE TAKEN IT OUT, NOW I'M PUTTING IT IN AGAIN, SO DON'T TELL ME THERE'S NO BLOODY DISK, OK?"

"Zere eez no disk een drive A."

"Look, is there anyone else I can talk to?"

Generally speaking man is still the master of the machines, except for when it comes to setting the timer on the video recorder. There was a scare a while back when the computer Deep Blue defeated Garry Kasparov at chess. The grandmaster had failed to make the most obvious move available to him, which was to lean across and pull the plug out. But there are various projects around the world that claim to have created genuine artificial intelligence. One team recently thought they'd cracked it when they asked their computer, "Can you recognise speech?" The machine said it could and proceeded to wreck a nice beach. And of course you can now buy electronic dictating programmes that put the words up on the screen as you say them. I actually use this software to write with and it works perflkadnl.

If computers are going to have the intelligence of humans, the worrying question is: Which particular humans are we talking about? What's the point of going to all that effort if all you produce is the electronic equivalent of some airhead pop star like Avril Lavigne? Or a palm-top with the mind of a politician? "What's Tim's address?" "Well, frankly, I don't think that is the question you should be asking here . . ." If the robots that make cars are given brains we'll be straight back in the seventies: mass walkouts and articles condemning the lazy American robot. With human sensibilities, computers will get all depressed about the meaningless of it all. "I'm not just some machine, you know." "Um, well, you are actually."

Why is it presumed that the most desirable form of artificial intelligence is one modelled on the human mind? If you want the computers to do as they're told it would be far better to recreate the thought processes of a golden retriever. As long as you could put up with the PCs smelling each others' modem ports, the machines would be far more dependable. You could take your computer to laptop obedience classes and say to the screen: "Stay . . . stay . . . and print!"

But scientists are determined to press on with trying to recreate what they consider to be the ultimate in artificial intelligence—a computer that thinks like a person. We will know that we've got there when we have a machine that really reasons, feels, and speaks like a normal human being. And then it'll say, "Actually, I don't understand most of the things on my computer. I just use it for typing letters really . . ."

THE SPIES WITH THE GOLDEN PENSION PLAN

17 March 2001

There was always a very good reason for spies demanding the utmost secrecy about the way they conducted their affairs. They were completely useless. They never caught any foreign agents; they just provided lots of free office space for spies working for the other side.

"Morning, Vladimir. I like your new sandwich box. Why's it got an aerial sticking out of the side?"

"Nyet, that is the handle, comrade, I mean, old chap."

But any questions about their effectiveness were always quashed for "reasons of security." It would be nice if we could all use this excuse to cover up how useless we are. "Darling, when you took the kids in to school today, you didn't forget their lunchboxes, did you?"

"Er—I am unable to discuss that for reasons of security."

"Oh—and I suppose you can't tell me if you remembered to get some milk on the way home?"

"Well, um, actually I can tell you that. But not until 2031."

John Major could have refused to reveal the outcome of the 1997 general election, attendance figures at the Millennium Dome could have been classified confidential, and sports journalists would've been reduced to writing, "England played Sweden today in a vital World

Cup qualifier, but the coach says he cannot reveal the result for reasons of security."

But now glasnost is grudgingly coming to Britain's security services. Former spy supremo Stella Rimmington is publishing her memoirs and this week her successor gave his first public speech since taking the job. Even the Parliamentary Intelligence and Security Committee is planning to hold some of its meetings in public, though I don't expect Andrew Lloyd Webber is too worried about the competition.

Of course the question politicians should be asking the head of the security services is "What are Britain's spies for?" That's the biggest secret of them all. You could understand it in the 1950s when everyone believed that those pesky Russians were plotting to invade the whole world and make us all wear furry hats and eat beetroot. We do still get the occasional war of course, and in its defence Britain's secret service was quick to discover the invasion of Kuwait when agents listened in to secret radio transmissions known as "the *Today* programme."

But while twenty-first-century Britain does not face any serious military threat, the security infrastructure remains intact. If our spies are not to be made redundant they should at least be redirected toward finding out the secrets that have eluded the rest of us for all these years. Like which bit is the pestle and which bit is the mortar? Why is only one company allowed to make "Monopoly"? Why has Princess Michael of Kent got a boy's name? Is she the same person as the Duchess of Kent and how does she get those free seats at Wimbledon? And if Britain doesn't have any enemies, who is there left for the secret agents to spy on? The answer is—British subjects, of course. This is nothing new; it was recently revealed that the government was spying on union activists during the 1970 dockers' strike. Throughout the 1980s, leaders of the campaign for nuclear disarmament had their mail opened, and militant union leaders had their phone tapped, which constitutes an outrageous breach of human rights: making someone listen to militant union leaders all day. No doubt the same undemocratic behaviour continues today, but for "reasons of security" there is no way of knowing who is targeted.

Spending on security services should have been reduced, but instead the spies have now got an ostentatious riverside property in central London. As part of the new spirit of openness they allowed this location to be used in a James Bond film in which terrorists fired missiles at their headquarters. At which point the IRA thought, "That's a good idea," and fired missiles at their headquarters. But the secret service is still dragging its heels on accountability because the more we find out about them the more obvious it becomes that they are an expensive waste of money. In reality 007 should be facing his toughest challenge yet: unemployment. James Bond is "The Spy Who Got Laid Off."

"Listen carefully, Bond. At first glance this piece of paper looks like an official form terminating your employment."

"Don't tell me—it folds out and releases a poisonous gas?"

"Nope, it *is* a piece of paper terminating your employment. On Monday morning you will go to your local Department of Social Security office."

"To collect my secret assignment to eliminate Iraqi terrorists?"

"No, to claim your jobseeker's allowance. Good luck, Bond."

Of course the right-wing press would go mad if all the spies were sacked but that's all right, the government wouldn't have to tell them. "For reasons of security," obviously.

MORE HOT AIR FROM
GEORGE BUSH

31 March 2001

I t's not that George W. Bush is ill-informed about the emission of greenhouse gases, but he can't understand why everyone doesn't just go into their greenhouses and close the windows.

"Yup, it's a kinda warm humid gas—smells of tomato plants and bags of fertiliser. But frankly I just don't see it as a threat to the future of the world."

By reneging on the United States' commitment to the Kyoto treaty on climate change, President Bush has signalled that the country is returning to isolationism, only this time he's decided that the United States won't be having anything to do with the rest of the world's weather. Like King Canute he thinks he is immune from the advancing seas. (Actually Canute was trying to demonstrate the opposite, but back in the eleventh century political spin was not as sophisticated as it is today.)

The timing of Bush's announcement seemed to be designed to bring maximum humiliation to the visiting Gerhard Schroeder. The German chancellor tried to put a brave face on it, saying that he and Bush had had a pleasant lunch and had found common ground on all issues except one. So they agreed to have sparkling water rather

than still, to share the medley of mixed vegetables and croquet pota-
toes, and the only sticking point was whether the United States
should honour its agreement to help prevent half the world's population from being underwater in a few years' time. Well, two out of
three's not bad. If they sat in the no-smoking section of the restaurant Dubya probably puffed on cigars throughout.

Bush was warned that the U.S. oil companies will now have to
face the wrath of Green Party Euro MPs. Boy, they must be worried.
The irony is of course that the Greens had it in their power to save
the Kyoto treaty. They knew that the environmental breakthrough
made by Clinton would not be supported by Bush. But they stood
against the Democratic Party anyway and as a direct result of that
decision the world's environment will now be affected for the worse.
Now we will have to wait until the Atlantic Ocean is lapping at the
knees of the Statue of Liberty before the U.S. government admits
there may possibly be a problem. The oil companies have their man
in the White House and are in complete control. He may be in the
driving seat but he's not going anywhere without gasoline. George
Bush's America has by far the greatest number of car owners in the
world. You'd think one of them could manage to run him over.

The news that global environmental policy is being dictated by
the oil multinationals is a fairly terrifying realisation. It'd be like
having an affirmative action programme being run by the Ku Klux
Klan. This is only the beginning. Now we can look forward to having peace talks being chaired by the arms manufacturers, the tobacco
companies being put in charge of cancer research, and the World
Health Organisation being chaired by Ronald McDonald. What is
so depressing about Bush's decision is that the rest of the world was
asking so little. The Kyoto treaty was far too timid in the first place
but this was because every concession was made to keep the world's
greatest polluters on board. Like negotiating with an aggressive drunk

in a pub, we could not have been more conciliatory, but the result
was always going to be the same:

"You spilt my beer."

"I'm sorry, I don't think I did . . ."

"You calling me a liar?"

"No of course not, let me buy you another one."

"Why are you trying to pick me up, you queer?"

"No, really; look, I'll leave. Why don't I leave the bar altogether?"

"Yeah, all right. Then I can follow you out and smash your face in."

So it is left to the other industrialised nations to save the world
from environmental catastrophe. Japan selflessly sent its economy
into a nosedive last week. Russia stopped functioning as a country
altogether a few years back. Meanwhile here in Britain every effort
has been made to prevent global warming. The railway companies
have turned off all the radiators in their waiting rooms. The owners
of mobile burger vans have been taking care to undercook hamburgers. Car owners have been driving around with rear screen heat-
ers that have several of the wires not working. Barbecues have been
left in the garden all winter so they are now filthy, rusty, and completely unusable. Despite Bush's selfish actions, in Britain everyone
has been doing their bit. Okay, so it's a shame all of England's efforts
have been completely cancelled out by the mass burning of farm
animals, but you can't have everything.

U R SCKD

20 May 2001

Yesterday it was announced that Ericsson, the Swedish mobile phone giant, is laying off ten thousand people. The chairman broke the news in the most sensitive manner possible. He sent all his employees a text message saying "U R sckd" followed by the symbol for a little sad face. For Sweden's traditional WAP handset-making community it marks the end of a way of life that goes all the way back to the late 1990s.

Suddenly the mobile phone bubble has burst. The downturn in sales has come as an enormous shock to everyone. No social trends analyst or marketing guru could have possibly foreseen that once everyone owned a mobile phone then sales of mobile phones might go down a little bit. The news has spread like wildfire: "Hi Mike, I've just got the figures—people are going off mobile phones, I can't understand it! Sorry, you're breaking up—I said people are going off mobile phones—I can't understand it. I SAID PEOPLE ARE GOING OFF MOBILE PHONES—I CAN'T UNDERSTAND IT— oh look, I'll ring you when I get to a land line."

Who could have possibly predicted that a fashion accessory would ever go out of fashion? Because that is the main reason that compa-

nies like Ericsson and Motorola have made their billions: their products were no more than the latest craze. Teenagers desperately needed
the most expensive communications technology so that they could
grunt monosyllables to one another. Parents, worried about the safety
of their children, were happy to fork out for a new handset, and then
their kids rang home in tears from a phone box to say they'd just been
mugged for their mobiles. Children carrying portable phones were
getting younger and younger. Toddlers riding on miniature steam
locomotives were getting out their mobiles and shouting "Ya, I'm on
a train. Ya, we're just going round the little goblin house, so I should
be back again in about thirty seconds."

But the trouble is that achieving sustained long-term growth when
you're flogging a fashion accessory is almost an impossibility. It was
the same for all those poor investors who staked their life savings on
platform shoes and purple tank tops in the mid-seventies. So the
industry has tried to move forward by providing more and more services. Now instead of one annoying ringing tone, you can choose
between dozens. These days no performance of *Romeo and Juliet* is
complete without a tinny rendition of the "William Tell Overture"
interrupting the most poignant moment. At soccer matches, every
goal is now followed by hundreds of beeps in the crowd, as everyone
receives text messages to inform them that their team has just scored.
(Maybe it's just me, but when I'm at a match and my team gets a goal
it's usually something I can't help noticing.) These developments
were followed with the new generation of high-tech, all-in-one handsets that were not just phones, they could also send e-mail, browse
the Internet, and trim unsightly nasal hair.

But although increased communication should be a wonderful thing,
I can't help worrying that the easier it becomes to relay information,
the less trouble will be taken with the content. When Moses came
down from the mountain with the Ten Commandments painstakingly

carved onto stone tablets, you get the sense that quite a lot of thought must have gone into how those messages should be expressed. If Moses had had a WAP phone he would have just forwarded the Almighty's e-mail that said "neighbour's ox: don't covet, love G." (Although being an old man, Moses might have got a bit nervous that the e-mail had actually got there, so he would have rung up everyone just to make sure.)

So it's hard to shed too many tears for the failure of the third generation of mobile phones. Though it has cost them billions, the mobile giants have discovered that when people are on the move they do not particularly want to surf the Internet—they can wait till they get home before they buy a wife from Russia. Now instead the phone companies will have to concentrate on breaking into less-developed markets, and already in Russia sales of yoghurt cartons and bits of string are doing great business. The important thing is that the government managed to get an absolute fortune out of the mobile phone companies for the new licenses before the bubble burst. It was the windfall tax for Labour's second term, even if all those billions are still not adequate compensation for having to listen to people shouting into their handsets on the train. And maybe I'm wrong, maybe this is just a blip, and before long we'll all be sending e-mails and surfing the Net on the way into the office that we weren't supposed to need anymore. In which case the government will need every single penny of those billions. The health service is going to be very busy after we have all tried speeding down the fast lane of the motorway and surfing the Internet at the same time.

NOT BEING PATRIOTIC: NO ONE DOES IT LIKE US BRITS

26 May 2001

Yesterday Tony Blair introduced his own brand of patriotism into the election campaign. The handling of this issue was debated long and hard and eventually Downing Street decided that a sensitive speech on the subject might come across better than the prime minister suddenly appearing with a Union Jack tattooed on his neck and singing "Eng-er-land! Eng-er-land!" Patriotism is always an awkward issue for the left—it asks the question, "Is it possible to be positive about your own country without somehow being negative about another?" I think the answer is that yes it is—unless you're French, of course.

A general election campaign gives us the opportunity to focus on what it is that we hold dear in this unique country of ours. Our picturesque English high streets peppered with their quaint little branches of Gap, Starbucks, and Dunkin' Donuts. The sound of Celine Dion blasting out of a Nissan Sunny as it screeches past the graffiti tags under the Daewoo hoarding. An evening spent at a Tex-Mex bar—sipping a Bud and watching the Miami Dolphins on Sky Sports Extra.

Patriotism is like germ warfare. I'd rather we didn't deploy it because it is so hideous when you see it used back on you by the other
side. One Conservative candidate is using his election address to
compare the European Union with Nazi Germany. Yes, all the aims
of the Brussels bureaucrats; it's all there in *Mein Kampf* if you take
the trouble to read Hitler's own words. Page 73: "Using this new lightning war we will defeat the inferior races of Europe and then we can
force them to list all food additives on the side of the jar." Page 174:
"The subhumans who are corrupting the Nordic master race must not
prevent us from fulfilling our Germanic destiny of setting a minimum
safety standard for all child car seats."

As we have already seen in this election, the flip side of the patriotism coin can be xenophobia. The status of asylum seekers is not
an issue that affects the everyday lives of any of us, and yet it was
built up as this terrible problem to try to appeal to the worst instincts
of the electorate. More voters have been inconvenienced by ants in
their kitchens than they have by asylum seekers but you never hear
politicians having a go at the ants. In fact insects generally is the one
issue that the politicians are too scared to face up to in this campaign.

Maybe this is the answer to the whole nationalism problem. If
we want humankind to love one another, irrespective of creed or
colour, we had better find ourselves some new enemies to have a go
at. Political debate has always depended upon an "us and them"
mentality—so when the world becomes one big harmonised international community we will have to stop being prejudiced against
other nations and direct our intolerance at other species instead.
Suddenly, callers on late-night radio phone-ins will be free to express
their opinions at will.

"Hello Brian, yeah, I want to talk about these bloody head lice
taking over our schools. You get one family of 'em and before you
know it they're everywhere. I tell you they're nothing but parasites."

"I'm not insectist, Brian, but these dung beetles—I'm sorry but they are dirty. They can't help it, it's just in their nature."

And the liberal on the panel will try to defend insects, saying the pictures in the tabloids are blowing the problem of carpet mites out of all proportion, but none of the callers will take any notice.

"Listen mate, my little girl just brushed past this wasp and it stung her on the arm—how do you defend that then?"

"Well, um, of course, er, there may be isolated cases where the behaviour of individual wasps might be unacceptable, but that doesn't mean we should hate *all* wasps . . ."

"Why not? I can't stand the little bastards."

Until this state of affairs comes about I am endeavouring to discriminate only against those who encourage discrimination. The trouble is that if we are too successful in our mission to wipe out the forces of bigotry, who are we going to be bigoted against? None of us are capable of loving everybody, except born-again Christians of course. And even they seem to see only the bad side of Satan.

SOME COKE WITH YOUR CHAMPAGNE?

16 June 2001

Few of those who were at Royal Ascot this week are actually at all interested in horse racing. You don't see many posh ladies with feathers and fruit bowls on their heads in my local bookmakers swearing and tearing up their betting slips as they blow the last few quid of the child benefit on the Kentucky Derby. Royal Ascot is a social pageant, a hat parade, a place to be obscenely rich and overheard. That's why they all wear those enormous hats: so that when someone's talking to you they can't look over your shoulder to see if there is someone more important standing behind. How the country managed to function without all these people at their desks is a mystery that will never be solved.

"Oh my God!" shouted Arabella suddenly. "I forgot to tell anyone at work that I wasn't coming in today! Who's going to tell the lady who arranges the flowers where to place her vase?"

"Pah!" said Rupert. "I told them straight; if any overseas clients want to bid for an antique clock via the Chelsea office, they'll just have to wait until Monday!" And there were gasps all around as his friends imagined the chaos Rupert's absence must have precipitated.

But this year's Ascot was tainted with the appalling news that cocaine was used inside the royal enclosure. Shock, horror; the idle rich taking cocaine?! Next they'll be avoiding tax and having it off with their nannies. For some reason this has been treated as an incredible revelation in some sections of the media. Somebody has held a mirror up to the British upper classes and they have snorted coke off it. And there was the Prince of Wales feeling so chuffed that all the posh girls kept saying how much they loved Charlie before announcing they were off to powder their noses. Now we know why the British royal family don't carry money. They got fed up with all their mates borrowing banknotes to roll up. Of course there's no suggestion that any member of the royal family themselves were taking any class A drugs, although the Queen Mother was overheard saying she felt "bloody brilliant" and had to be physically prevented from attempting to outrun the horses racing in the 4.20.

But it's a shame that a minority of cokeheads have to spoil a lovely day out by consuming a recreational drug reserved for the super-rich, when the vast majority of law-abiding visitors just want to pass the day drinking bottles of vintage champagne. Why do these people feel a need to escape from reality when they were pretty well removed from it before they even started? The sociologists have tried to be as sensitive as possible:

"Look, rather than just condemning these drug users, let's try to understand them. I mean some of these kids off the estates may never work again. And now they've even lost their parents' trust. Or rather, they've spent it."

Maybe cocaine use has always been used at race meetings; that would explain why the commentators always talk so quickly. With all those drugs do the jockeys' multicoloured shirts just blend into the psychedelic background? But there were also reports of cocaine

at other race meetings this year. It's not known if any of the horses
actually took cocaine, although suspicions were aroused halfway
through one race when the horses started to flag and then disappeared
into the toilets before coming back out wiping their noses and rar-
ing to go again.

No doubt the police will be as tough on drug users at Royal Ascot
as they would be on any inner-city housing project. It's the dealers
they are really after; so anyone driving an expensive car into the
enclosure was pulled over and questioned.

"This is a fancy ride, sunshine; what's your name then?"

"The Duke of Wellington."

"Yeah, and I'm bloody Napoleon—don't get fresh with me sonny,
or you'll be chucked in the back of the police van with that bloke
who said he was the Sultan of Brunei."

The police should adopt a zero tolerance approach to drug-taking
at race meetings. Rows of police horses should line up and charge
the dealers.

"Great idea!" said Rupert . . . "and like, there could be a prize for
the horse that comes first and you could place bets on who you think
will win . . ."

Except no one would be watching, of course, they'd all be in the
corporate tents getting out of their heads on cocaine. Anyway you
couldn't have two meetings at the same place; it's simple arithmetic,
even a cokehead could tell you that two into one won't go. Coke
addicts' nostrils excepted of course.

DUBYA GETS HIS FIRST PASSPORT

23 June 2001

This week George W. Bush came to Europe, and before setting off he was given a full and detailed briefing.

"It's a kinda big peninsular, Mr. President, with lots of different countries in it."

"Sounds great—how come I never went before?"

"Well sir, with respect, you never had a passport till now."

There was a slight delay at the airport check-in desk when Bush said, "No, of course I didn't pack this bag myself. I'm president of the United States." Then airport security couldn't work out why the metal detectors kept bleeping every time his bodyguards walked through. So they put their keys in the little bowl, then their loose change, and eventually their semiautomatic machine guns, and that finally seemed to do the trick.

The reason that George W. has flown across the Atlantic is to get to know his allies in NATO and the EC. The plan was that they would meet the new president face-to-face and then feel reassured. Some ideas are flawed from the very outset. Of course when any new world leader joins the club he or she is slightly vulnerable and because Bush's understanding of foreign affairs is rather limited the various European leaders decided to have a bit of fun with him. Just when he thought he'd worked out who was leader of which country, the European heads of state secretly swapped nationalities just for a laugh. Tony Blair started speaking French, smoking Gitanes, and claiming that the Second World War was won by the French resistance. Jacques Chirac spoke German and drank frothy lager from a two-litre stein. Silvio Berlusconi looked on sipping his Guinness and singing "Danny Boy." A confused Bush turned to Jose Maria Aznar to clarify things but the Spanish prime minister just said something in Dutch and offered him a joint. This joke is set to backfire when Bush goes to Jerusalem and meets Ariel Sharon and says, "Stop having me on— you're the Palestinian guy, right?"

Dinner was then served for the fifteen heads of state. The president was treated to the finest Italian wine and delicious French food, all rounded off with a traditional English speciality, spotted dick and custard. The Europeans agreed it was wonderful to see such a brilliant American president who combined political integrity with determination and compassion. Then they stopped talking about *The West Wing* and concentrated on more urgent matters. They tried to raise the issue of the environment but George didn't seem to get it. Even when he'd been asked to choose his trout from the fish tank he'd failed to notice anything unusual when all the fish were dead and floating in a little oil slick. They raised the missile defence shield project and claimed that he wasn't listening to their concerns but he just nodded and said "Yup, and this sauce is delicious too."

Bush talks about rogue states, but on Kyoto and missile defence, it is America that is behaving like a rogue state. He is stockpiling weapons of mass destruction and the UN has not been allowed to inspect any of them. Of course the European leaders would have liked to announce sanctions such as an official boycott of McDonald's; it's just that their kids keep nagging them for the free plastic toys. It leaves you wondering what is the point of having a closer European Union if it is not prepared to use its combined strength to stand up to the world's only superpower. Would America proceed with missile defence in the face of unified opposition from Europe? Would Bush have torn up the Kyoto treaty if it meant enduring the wrath of the world's largest trading bloc? Er, yes he would, but that's not the point.

Bush may not care what Europe thinks, but if its leaders were a little more direct and frank in their opposition at least they might salvage a little pride and dignity from the situation. This applies to the British government more than any other. Britain can't be a bridge between Europe and the United States and be at the heart of Europe as well. Tony Blair rang George W. Bush after he was inaugurated to check that the special relationship would be unchanged. The lady on the White House switchboard logged the call and said, "Have a nice day Mr. Blur," so yup, it's pretty much as before.

Europe needs to show some leadership because the official leader of the western world is leading the world in the wrong direction. He's fallen for the American military's arguments and restarted the arms race. Bush says he was only persuaded to proceed with the Star Wars project after a full intelligence assessment. Well quite; they did one and found he doesn't have any.

CHOOSE THE SEX OF
YOUR CHILD

7 July 2001

A doctor in America has just invented a "sperm sorting machine." At least that's what he claimed when his receptionist burst into the office to find him doing something peculiar with the Hoover attachment. Either way a clinic in the United States is now charging the modest fee of $2,000 in order to allow couples to choose the sex of their child. This development would have provoked the major moral dilemma of our age, were it not for all the other major moral dilemmas currently piling up in the in-tray. Should we allow the cloning of humans? Should we permit euthanasia? When you receive a written invitation, is it okay to RSVP by phone?

The world would be very different if parents had always had this choice. Imagine if Lady Thatcher's father had chosen to have a son. Our first woman prime minister might have been an aggressive warmongering politician instead of the gentle loving woman she turned out to be. Ahem. Or what if Arnold Schwarzenegger's parents had chosen a girl? "She" would have beaten up a dozen mutants, fired off her rocket launcher, and destroyed the cybercity and everyone would have said, "You know, evening primrose oil can sometimes help with PMS, dear." It's hard to know if your parents always secretly hoped you'd be born the opposite sex, although if I were Princess Michael of Kent I'd be a bit suspicious. Most couples always pretend that they don't mind what sex their baby will be. When people said to Anne Boleyn, "What do you want: a boy or girl?" she said "Well a girl would be nice because I could buy her dolls and dresses and things. But then part of me hopes it's a boy because otherwise Henry will chop my head off." But now at last the ability to choose is a genuine reality. Couples who've had several children of the same sex will now be able to balance it out a bit. *Seven Brides for Seven Brothers* will be remade as *Seven Partners For Various Siblings of Alternate Sexes*.

The system used for separating the male and female sperm is remarkably simple. The sample is placed in a petri dish with a microscopic pile of household items on a tiny staircase. All the sperm that go straight past without picking anything up are obviously boys. Fertilization is then just a scientific formality. Of course, before in vitro fertilization the long journey to the egg was fraught with difficulty. The male sperm just whizzed around all over the place hoping to find it, while the female sperm kept saying they should stop and ask someone. Eventually the male sperm suggested that she map-read and then he got all cross because she had to hold the map upside down to get her bearings.

Of course some have argued that so much preplanning should not go into a child's life before conception. Soon pregnant mothers will be going around saying "It's a boy, he's an Aries, and he's a borough surveyor." Soon it will be possible to choose not only the sex of your baby but the social class as well. Working-class moms will find little Drusilla saying things like "Mother—I want Nanny to take me to the gymkhana. It was so embarrassing last time when you mixed up a colt with a gelding." And instead of just dressing their middle-class kids up in miniature denim jackets and tiny steel-tipped boots, right-on parents will order a bona fide working-class son complete with skin-head haircuts and tattoos. And they'll watch him playing with his wooden blocks and proudly say, "Oh look, he's going to be a labourer when he grows up."

The news that we are now able to select the gender of our children was greeted with the usual hand-wringing. Some commentators said, "It is time we had a full public debate on this whole area," which is another way of saying "I haven't the faintest idea what I think about this one." Meanwhile there were the predictable howls of outrage from the very quarters that are always banging on about freedom of choice. Because while we're confronted with too much choice when it comes to movie channels and different sizes of cappuccino, for the really big things in life the right's instinct is to deny people real choices. Why shouldn't parents be able to opt for the gender they would prefer? Who could it harm apart from the people selling yellow babygrows? Either way when the child is born the choices will still be narrow enough.

Maybe the critics don't like new generations having the opportunities that they never had. Perhaps they feel that IVF makes it all too effortless. "Honestly, sperm today, they have it so easy," they say. "When I was a sperm, it was a struggle; no fancy doctors helped me reach the egg, I did it through my own hard work and perseverance. But young sperm these days, they don't know they're born. Oh, they're not, are they?"

AFTER YOU WITH
THE TROUGH

28 July 2001

This week a survey revealed that the average British chief executive now takes home half a million a year, not including bonuses, share options, and those Post-it notes that he nicked from the office stationery cupboard. Defenders of the very rich say that the criticism of these enormous boardroom salaries is based on envy and class hatred. And they say it as if this is a bad thing.

Boardroom salaries first soared after the famous Company Director's Strike back in 1982. Who can forget those dramatic scenes as angry mobs of pinstriped businessmen fought pitched battles outside the stock exchange? Food convoys were organised to bring them four-course lunches from L'Escargot. Violence erupted as they got their chauffeurs to overturn cars. Mounted policeman rushed up to the strikers, saying, "Are you all right there, sir?" After months of bitter struggle a complex pay settlement was agreed to and executive salaries are now decided on the following criteria: the chairmen say to themselves, "What's the most outrageous and exorbitant pay raise I can give myself? Right, I'll have that much then."

Even companies that are laying off staff still seem to find the money to pay huge bonuses to the board. Last year the chairman of Vodafone took an award of £13 million. I know it sounds like a lot, but really by the time you've paid the accountants and the tax man it's actually only around £12 million. And now the only good causes that are getting more money from the National Lottery are the directors' own bank accounts. It leaves you wondering why these greedy people need so much money. If I were a multimillionaire, I wouldn't want much more than I have now. All I'd buy is a nice house with a bigger garden and that would be it. And I suppose if I've got all that garden I might as well have a swimming pool in it. And a tennis court, and there could be, like, a little stream with a bridge and a path that leads down to the orchard. But apart from that, oh and the cars, and the flat in town, and the villa in Tuscany, my needs would be modest.

There is an unhealthy fascination with the lifestyles of the super-rich that needs to be countered with some positive publicity for the people at the other end of the pay scale. There should be special magazines in which skint ex-soldiers invite the cameras in to see their cockroach infested bed-sit. And the newspapers should publish a "Sunday Times Poor List"—"This week we list Britain's 100 most impoverished plebs; at number 57 is Fat Degsy of Urine Towers, Rotherham, whose assets include a half an ounce of rolling tobacco and a beard. Total value 34 pence. But he's still much richer than the couple who've just gone straight in at number one; congratulations to the chairman of Bosnia Adventure Tours Limited!"

Just as Britain's poorest have formed an underclass, so the very rich are excluded from society as an "overclass." They do not use the schools, hospitals, trains, or anything else that might involve the horrors of mixing with ordinary people, or even worse, queueing. These poor people are outcasts from society; they need all the help and support we can give them so that they can start to live normal lives once again.

What is needed is a new windfall tax to be levied on the fat cats. This suggestion is based purely on economic grounds and is certainly not prompted by any sort of left-wing bitterness. Anyway, the so-called Rich Bastard Tax would involve a £10,000 tariff on anything that the newly appointed "Snob Tsar" deemed to be "vulgar, ostentatious, or just annoyingly wealthy." Personalized number plates would be a good place to start—I don't see why these don't just all say "2 MUCH MONEY." There'd be a surcharge for anyone driving a Porsche with a sticker on the back saying "My other car's a Porsche." Second homes would be another good target, and the tax would be doubled if the owners were overheard referring to them as "just a little bolt-hole in the country." Rolex watches, automatic garage doors, Moschino handbags, or any clothes bought from a shop where you have to ring a bell to be let in; all sorts of things would warrant the extra duty. I'd like to put in a personal plea to surcharge the owner of that £100,000 cabin cruiser I saw on the River Thames that was called "Just a Whim."

"Ah but it's not that simple . . ." says the government. "Tackling these fat cats is a very tough job indeed. It's going to need the very best people to see it through, a cabinet of the highest calibre, who won't be tempted to get better paid jobs elsewhere. So we're all agreed then, ministers; we'll just award ourselves a massive pay increase before we get started."

PRODUCT PLACEME*N*T S*ICKE*NS ME

4 August 2001

his week saw the biggest argument in Hollywood since E.T. quit the movie business claiming he was always being typecast as a loveable alien.

"I am a serious actor! I can do Shakespeare, look: To be, or not beee goood, Damn! Damn!"

The latest scandal to rock Tinseltown is over a product placement deal for the film *American Pie 2*. You may have been unfortunate enough to catch the original that is endlessly reshown on the Sky Puerile Movies Channel, which is famous for a scene in which an adolescent boy has sex with an apple pie. Obviously this is not something any normal person should ever attempt, as I said to that doctor at the burns clinic next door to McDonald's.

In the sequel, the teenagers actually graduate to having sex with each other, and to the filmmakers' credit, the sex is safe. No condoms were featured in the original film, which led to criticism that the boy could have been infected by one of the apple pie's previous lovers. This time round the money men at Universal Studios thought they'd spotted the chance for some lucrative product placement, and struck a deal with the manufacturers of Lifestyle condoms, which would feature prominently in the movie (presumably before they were put on, or that Parental Guidance certificate would have been a real long shot). The studio also undertook to promote the Lifestyle brand in the adverts for *American Pie 2*, but instead of honouring the deal, Universal pulled out prematurely, which as we all know is no substitute for using a condom.

It turns out that American regulations prohibit condoms featuring in any commercials that might be seen by a general audience. Car chases, shoot-outs, and robberies are fine, but mention contraception and you have crossed the boundary of good taste. Which is bizarre because sex has always been used to sell films. Although at least in *Last Tango in Paris* they didn't feel the need to establish what brand of butter it was.

The controversy has highlighted the whole issue of product placement: the prominent featuring of brand names as a form of oblique advertising. Somehow you sense that the great films of the past would not have had quite the same impact if directors like David Lean had depended on covert advertising. When Alec Guinness staggers out of that baking little cell in *Bridge on the River Kwai*, he does not say:

"Well thank goodness I had my Right Guard double protection."

"Why 'double' protection, sir?"

"Because it protects your noses and your clothes-es."

"Yes, and I should add, sir, that this prison camp is much better since it got taken over by Club Med."

"Indeed, the men's morale has been greatly lifted by the pedalo race down the River Kwai."

Some might argue that the opening of Bergman's 1957 classic *The Seventh Seal*, in which Antonius Block encounters the figure of Death, might have been improved if instead of embarking on a game of chess they had played with the free plastic toys now being given out with McDonald's Happy Meals. "If your little clockwork turtle goes across the table quicker than mine I shall release you." "And if

I lose?" "Then . . ." says Death, "you'll have to let me finish your Chocolate McMilkshake."

Or what about the moment in *Casablanca* when Ilsa walks into Rick's place. All the agony of Bogart's broken heart is written on his face when suddenly the silence is broken by a waitress saying to Ilsa, "Hello, welcome to TGI Friday's."

The trouble is that some films are easier to get sponsors for than others. Few were surprised when the cruise ship companies decided not to have their name splashed all over *Titanic*. Of course art needs financial backing; this has been going on ever since the money men persuaded Shakespeare to do a sequel to *Henry IV Part One*, but product placement can only diminish the integrity and quality of a film. Furthermore if a studio has been paid millions of dollars to show the hero drinking Budweiser, then the editor is duty bound to leave in that scene however bad it is and however it affects the rest of the movie.

So now you go to the cinema and you are jolted out of your enjoyment of the film every time a global brand is shoved in your face; every time the star pointedly pulls on his Gap sweatshirt and Nike trainers or the camera lingers on his bottle of Miller Draft or his new Nokia communicator. But there's a reason that the corporations have to promote their wares so crassly within the body of the main feature. It's because before the film proper you have to sit through a dozen arty pretentious commercials and at the end of each one you turn to your friends and say, "What was that an advert for?" And they reply, "I haven't the faintest idea."

CLONE-AGE MAN

11 August 2001

The British government recently gave the go-ahead for the cloning of human embryos. To illustrate this story the newspapers published the magnified image of a fertilized cell, prompting a flurry of calls from Downing Street to check that it wasn't an intrusively early photo of Tony Blair's baby. The decision was announced by science minister Lord Sainsbury, and after a quick glance over the press release, journalists carelessly dashed off the surprising story, "Sainsbury Supermarkets to Make Human Embryos Available."

This was an announcement that has been coming ever since the birth of Dolly the Sheep. Dolly, as the first ovine clone, caused a media sensation a few years back, but has since rather failed to keep hold of the public's attention. She's just sacked her publicity manager and is now planning a relaunch as soon as she gets out of the Betty Ford Clinic. As soon as the concept of cloning human embryos was given the green light, the religious right started foaming at the mouth, while at the BBC the producers of the *Moral Maze* simply passed out with the excitement.

Opponents of these developments warn of a nightmare world in which whole groups of people would be exactly the same. It's almost impossible to imagine—Republican candidates who were all identical white male former investment bankers. GIs who all have the same physique, tattoos, and crew-cuts. It doesn't bear thinking about. "God in his wisdom made each of us totally unique," said every single religious leader last week.

In the 1970s film *The Boys from Brazil*, it transpires that Nazi scientists have cloned a whole batch of young Adolf Hitlers whom they're grooming to become the new führer to take over the entire world, or failing that, the DMV. The film was a somber warning as to how science can go badly wrong, causing people to talk in unconvincing German accents and grow bizarre wonky moustaches. But who else might be recreated now that this technology is genuinely available? Perhaps in our lifetime we will be able to visit a historical theme park, where cloned figures from history will show us round the attractions. "Welcome to the Gettysburg Experience!" the clone of Abe Lincoln will say. "No photos please; if you want any souvenirs just ask Genghis Khan there in our gift shop." Perhaps Marilyn Monroe will be on the till if she's not locked in the storeroom with the clone of John F. Kennedy.

Most of the biologists making these breakthroughs are motivated only by a desire to save human lives. Many of them feel they have been misrepresented in the media, though when I phoned one of them about this, his assistant Igor said the master was busy up on the roof with the lightning conductor. Their great breakthrough was apparently the discovery of "stem" cells. These are the cells that give chemical messages to other cells telling them to develop into a particular type of tissue. This is less reliable with male cells, as they always forget to pass on the message. Some cells turn into bone, some cells turn into brain, the unlucky ones turn into that bit of skin on your Adam's apple that you always cut when you're shaving. Soon biologists hope to be able to inject the appropriate cells to help the body produce its own tissue of exactly the desired type. This has the potential to help everyone from diabetics to people with damaged internal organs. Even new limbs could be grown, although it may be too late to help the current England soccer team.

The scientists are using fertilised cells that would perish anyway to help people who are already alive. An embryo is not a foetus, which is not a baby. The moment of fertilisation is just one milestone in the creation of human life; it is one of the stages in a long and gradual development to that joyful moment when a baby pops out and keeps you awake for two years. The embryos used in this research are less than a week old. Most couples will have lost fertilised cells without even knowing it before one finally attached itself to the wall of the womb and made its host start bursting into tears and eating pickled onions and ice cream. The people who find the whole idea of cloning human embryos distasteful would probably prefer to put Alzheimer's and cancer in the back of their minds as well. This is a huge leap forward and the church's reaction was depressing in its predictability. Now I understand why they were always against the cloning of Dolly. We don't need any more sheep when we already have the religious right bleating the same old objections.

The Bible actually says that God made man in his own image but really this is just not specific enough. Does God look like Leonardo di Caprio or like Danny De Vito? If God made Rush Limbaugh in his own image then frankly you'd have to question his judgment. There are certain personalities that make you want to rush through a bill preventing there being any more of them. One Pat Buchanan is already more than enough.

Although the production of human clones remains illegal in Britain and in America, it still seems likely to happen soon somewhere in the world. All the visitors will gather around the hospital bed and say, "Aaaah—he looks just like his dad."

"Yes, that's because he *is* his dad."

And the poor woman who has just given birth to the baby version of her husband will say, "What about the eyes? They're a bit like mine, aren't they?"

"Er—not really—I'd say he has his dad's eyes, ears, nose—well, everything really."

This week an Italian couple announced that they plan to have a baby that is a clone of the "father," and the maverick doctor Severino Antinori has confirmed that the first human clone is only months away. It has always been part of the human experience to gradually realise that you are turning into your parents, but this poor child will never stand a chance. Every time he slurps his drink his mother will say, "Well you get that from your father. And mixing your peas up with your mash, you get that from him as well. And picking your nose and hunching your shoulders and of course you'll never buy your wife flowers or take her on a luxury cruise like she always wanted."

And Dad'll say, "Leave him alone, he's a good lad. He just never got the breaks in life."

"Well he's only five."

Then when the child becomes a teenager the problems will really start. The boy will look at his dad, and filled with anger and disgust will shout, "I'm never going to be like you" and the parents will glance at each other and say, "Do you want to tell him or shall I?" Then he'll learn that one day, he too will wear cardigans and want to look inside churches on holiday. And the poor boy will explode and shout, "I hate you!"

"No darling, you can't hate me because I love you, and since I am you, *you* must love you too so in fact you love me, don't I?"

That should keep him quiet for a while.

The imminence of a human clone this week prompted the French health minister to say that we cannot permit "the photocopying of human beings." It is indeed a terrifying thought. Just imagine it— you'd be queueing up at the cloning machine all ready to make a hundred copies and the girl behind you would say, "Do you mind if I just pop in front of you, I'm only doing one clone."

So you let her in, and isn't it always the way—the machine jams.

"Oh dear, what's happened? The fault code is flashing 'J8'—Does anybody know what 'J8' means?"

"Is that 'Stem cells jammed in copier'?"

"Er—copier out of DNA?"

"It can't be—I put in a new amino proteins cartridge this morning."

"Oh no—I've got a hundred clones to do before lunch. Now I'm going to have to pop down to Kinko's to do them."

The advances in stem cell technology have until now been rightly justified on the grounds that they are helping prevent diseases. Similarly everything should be done to help childless couples have babies. But to create a human being who was already someone else is an abuse of the human rights of that newborn individual. It is one thing to clone a sheep, because the life choices facing sheep are pretty limited. Most lambs come out of their careers interview at school and say to their anxious parents, "Brilliant news! He thinks he might be able to get me into the wool business!" And mom and dad jump up and down with delight that all the hopes they had for their clever offspring will be realised: she's going to stand around in a wet field for a few months and then be served up as lamb chops.

But how is any person supposed to live a normal life with the knowledge that they are a duplicate of someone, possibly a "parent"; how are they supposed to become an individual in their own right?

It must be hard enough joining the family business without having "Johnson and Clone" on the side of the van. World leaders should act now to prevent human cloning. I cannot understand why they are dragging their feet. Do they imagine they could use this power and clone themselves so that they can govern forever and ever? George Bush is doing little to prevent it, as did his father George Bush. Oh no, I've just had a terrifying realisation. . . .

THE SCIENTISTS ARE MAKING IT ALL UP

18 August 2001

As news stories go, this item has taken slightly longer to reach the front pages than most, but the scientific journal *Nature* has just published an exclusive that four million years ago Earth was involved in an enormous interplanetary collision. The story was immediately picked up by all the papers, which each put their own particular spin on it. *Le Monde:* "Earth in Cosmic Collision; Bush and Blair to Blame." *The New York Post:* "Bang!" *The Des Moines Register:* "Interplanetary Crash Created Solar System. No One From Des Moines Involved."

The revelation that a protoplanet the size of Mars crashed into Earth, tilting Earth's polar axis and accelerating our orbit, has caused great excitement in the scientific world and given insurance companies another excuse to put up their premiums. It turns out that before the collision, Earth had a day that was only five hours long. So you'd stay up for two days and two nights and then sleep straight through for a couple of days—it was like being on holiday in Cancun. The collision sent billions of tons of molten rock into the atmosphere, which typically the weather forecasters of the time failed to spot:

"A lady rang in to say that molten gravel and flaming rocks will be raining down for the next million years—don't worry, they won't be; though do look out for a little light drizzle over the West Country over the weekend," said the weatherman, as lumps of molten lava landed all around him. Some of the debris from the collision flew up into space and eventually coalesced to form the satellite we know as the moon, later joined by other satellites sent into orbit by a powerful force known as Rupert Murdoch.

It was previously believed that the moon was created by a white-haired man called God on a Tuesday, but as cosmology has become more advanced, this theory has failed to withstand rigorous scientific scrutiny. The collision theory is not an entirely new one but now there are detailed computations that have apparently proved it. On page 709 of this week's *Nature*, the scientists explain how they made their calculations: "We use a beta spine kernel," they say. Oh yeah, right, a beta spine kernel. Pull the other one. There are then two full pages of mathematical calculations and equations involving lots of Greek letters and squiggly symbols that they knew the subeditor would take one look at and say, "Er, yup, that all looks fine!"

Clearly what has happened is that the scientists are making this all up. They have obviously spent the last two years sending each other silly e-mails and playing Minesweeper and when their deadline suddenly came along, they were forced to throw together a scientific theory and some calculations so they didn't get into trouble.

"Okay, quick, quick: when shall we say this happened?"

"I dunno—500 million years ago?"

"No no—bigger numbers are more impressive. Say four and a half billion."

"Okay, and say it was really, really hot—that always sounds good."

"Yeah, and make sure we use the words 'atoms,' 'gravity,' 'unstable,' and, er, 'beta spine kernel.'"

"What's beta spine kernel?"

"Three random words from the dictionary. Don't worry—no one will question it."

Making things up about space has been a huge industry ever since Richard Nixon decided that the moon landings were a complete waste of money and that the same images could be produced far more cheaply in a Hollywood back lot. The account of what really happened back in 1969 is only just coming out, but it was not much different from any other film set.

"Okay Neil darling, you step off your ladder and you say your line about the giant leap for mankind . . . and action!"

"But what's my motivation for going down the ladder? What's the back story here?"

"Cut! Oh no, not this again. Neil, love, you're playing an astronaut. You're landing on the moon. It's a big day for your character."

"Maybe I should drive around the moon in a big car?"

"No, darling—that's in the sequel, 'Apollo 12.'"

"Or lose radio contact and nearly die."

"'Apollo 13.'"

And the guys from NASA were sulking in the wings saying, "It can't be that difficult to do this for real. After all we've put a man on the moon."

"No we haven't."

"Well, no, but it's not rocket science."

"Yes it is."

Before science accounted for the creation of Earth and the moon, it was explained in the first chapter of the Bible. It didn't sound very believable but their get-out clause was that you had to have faith.

Now religion has been replaced with science and we just have to take someone else's word for it instead. The comforting thing is that at least we no longer live in fear of flaming thunderbolts coming out of the sky if we question the word of the Almighty. Well, not until they've got the Star Wars project up and running anyway.

WELCOME TO ENGLAND; SMACKING AREA— 200 YARDS

8 September 2001

Under proposals unveiled this week, Scotland is set to make the smacking of young children illegal for the first time in the UK. Dinnertime in Edinburgh will never be the same.

"I'm not eating my vegetables—they've got black bits in them."

"DO YOU WANT ME TO DRIVE YOU OVER THE BORDER AND GIVE YOU A SMACK?"

They'll have to build a special lay-by just after the bridge saying "Welcome to England; Smacking Area—200 yards." Little stalls will spring up selling brussels sprouts and broccoli and stationery for writing thank-you letters for Auntie's birthday present.

The plan is to ban the smacking of children under three, so now instead of saying, "Wait till your father gets home," toddlers will be told, "Just you wait until your third birthday." But the proposals have received a surprisingly positive response in the tough projects of Glasgow. In response to the question "Do you think parents should

be allowed to give their kids a little smack?" most people answered
"No, maybe just a bit of crack cocaine every now and then."

Of course smacking has only been the symptom of a historical
problem—this ruling will do nothing to prevent the recurrent breakdown of negotiations between adults and their offspring. If the Scottish government is ruling out the use of force then clearly more efforts
will have to be made on the diplomatic front. The first step should
be sporting sanctions. Parents will continue to play soccer with their
children but they will no longer be prepared to let their kids always
win. "And the final score here from Jamie's back garden: Dad 27, little
Jamie nil! And the six-year-old must surely be wishing now that he
hadn't been rude to Grandma back when he was four." Games of hide-
and-seek will be much quicker as parents find their children in under
three seconds. "It's no good crying, Ellie; you've hidden behind that
curtain four times in a row—of course I was going to look there first."
Because if punishment is not to be physical then it will have to be
psychological. "Night-night, Rosie. And darling, you know you were
scared that there was a great big bear that lived behind the cupboard
on the landing. Well you're right, there is: a huge fierce one with big
sharp teeth and long claws! Anyway, sweet dreams darling." Other
sanctions will include seizure of all comfort blankets and being honest about how crappy their drawings are.

But eventually the civilised example of Scotland will spread to
the rest of the country, if only because government ministers find
it impossible to negotiate with children's representatives. "At Downing Street today, talks have broken down between the preschool
children and the government. A draft proposal was put before the
toddlers, but they reacted by scribbling on it and then putting it in and
out of the water jug. When ministers objected, the two-year-olds
lay on the floor kicking and screaming and then fell asleep on the
rug." Before Westminster is prepared to follow the Scottish example

more concessions must be made from young children. If no violence is to be used against toddlers then they must undertake not to climb into bed at two in the morning and kick their dads in the bollocks. And it is no good them merely promising not to strike their little sisters with the plastic sword; their arms must be put permanently beyond use. Super Soakers, spud guns, sharp bits of Lego left beside the bed; all these weapons must be decommissioned before the peace process can really proceed. But eventually it will be illegal to give a child a light slap on the back of the hand (unless they are Iraqi kids of course; you'll still be allowed to drop bombs on them).

In the meantime, if you are tempted to strike a child in anger, they say you should make yourself count to ten first. This either prevents you from using violence or results in your child growing up into a neurotic adult with an irrational fear of double figures. All parents will know that there are times when it feels as if smacking your child is the only possible response—like when they announce that Barney the dinosaur is better than *The Simpsons*. But even if a quick slap seems to work in the short term, there has to be a better way of punishing them. Wait till they're teenagers and meet them at school in purple-checked golfing trousers. Visit them at university wearing a fur coat and a tiara. Wait till they have kids of their own and give your grandchildren a slush-puppy and a king-size Mars bar before they go on the Big Dipper. And keep endlessly telling your kids, "We never smacked you as a child, and that's why you're not a violent person." And then our grown-up children will say, "I know I shouldn't really hit my parents, but sometimes it's the only thing that works."

PRINCE EDWARD—
STALKER LAUREATE

29 September 2001

The media should leave Prince William alone. His arrival at university should barely be reported. Obviously, intelligent critiques on media intrusion are excepted; it's important for commentators such as myself to examine the conflict between private life and public duty, but that is the only valid reason for even mentioning Prince William in the newspapers right now. Anyway, doesn't he look like his mom? Aaah bless him, I hope he settles in all right; I wonder if he'll get a girlfriend? More pictures, pages 7, 8, and 9.

This week Prince Edward's TV production company was lambasted for filming Prince William without permission. Edward has clearly forgotten the words of Diana's brother at her funeral. Maybe this was because he was secretly videoing it for release on Exclusive Royal DVDs, a great Christmas gift at only £12.99. It's one thing for the paparazzi to be caught trying to film Prince William, but for a modern-day royal to attempt to cash in on his royal connections—it would be like Vlad the Impaler buying shares in Stakes 'R' Us.

Apparently Prince Charles is beside oneself with anger. It is in fact possible that Prince Edward has unwittingly ensured that his nephew's university life will remain private for the time being.

Which if we're really honest is a bit of a shame because it would have been quite entertaining to watch the everyday life of a royal undergraduate.

"Now listen, young man, if you don't work hard and get a good degree, you'll never get a decent job, will you?"

"Yes I will. I'm going to be king."

"Er, well yes, but er, you'll still need to earn a living before then."

"No I won't."

"Er, well no, but that aside, we're going to treat you like any other student. So here's your first essay: two thousand words please answering the question 'So what do you really think of Camilla?'"

William is studying the history of art but his comments in his first tutorial apparently showed he was a little confused. "It's amazing how Van Dyke managed to do that picture of Charles I while balancing on a stepladder peering over the palace wall. And Holbein's eyesight must have been fantastic—the picture of Anne of Cleves has amazing detail considering he didn't have a telephoto lens."

If Prince Edward's cameras had never been spotted, we could have seen William in the student production of *Waiting for Godot*, with that memorable scene where the tramp wanders out alone onto the bare stage followed by seven special branch security officers. We could have watched him break the college record on the rugby pitch as the opposing players decide against jumping on him whilst all those police marksmen were taking aim up in the trees. We could have seen him get up to all the usual undergraduate high jinks: sneaking into his friend's bedroom and getting his butler to make them an apple pie bed. The late nights sitting on the floor and talking about life, as the maid brings in a silver tray with mugs of blobby coffee; all of this will take place in private. Or perhaps the real reason Charles doesn't want William filmed is that he doesn't want everyone witnessing the embarrassing period when his undergraduate son goes all left-wing, arguing for the abolition of the monarchy and desperately trying to play down his privileged background.

"Actually my family isn't that well off; we got Windsor Castle when property prices were much lower. And we had to do loads of work on it, especially after the War of the Roses."

And he'll cringe when dad phones to say he's coming to visit. "Well don't all arrive in the big ostentatious Sikorsky. Come in the little helicopter. And tell Granny not to wear her crown."

Poor William is as desperate to be a normal student as Edward is to run a normal production company. In the old days there were pretenders to the throne. Now the royals pretend to be commoners. But Uncle Edward can't remain a royal and monopolise broadcast access to the royals. Since his company has always struggled, Edward should now return to state duties. A new position in the royal household needs to be created: Edward should be appointed the "Stalker Laureate"—official harasser and invader of the Royal Family's privacy. "The strange man who got inside the royal apartments today turned out to be the queen's youngest son. Police found pictures of the Countess of Wessex in his wallet and said he had regularly been filmed trying to get into royal residences." Edward might even find his celebrity status back up with the rest of them. Then the only problem would be stopping him from making a documentary about himself.

LACK OF IDENTITY CARDS

6 October 2001

When identity cards were brought in by the BBC, a comedy producer I knew decided to test the system by making a few changes to his pass. For a while he was waved through without question. Then one eagle-eyed security officer called him back. The guard took a good look at the photo on the card, which featured a shady man wearing sunglasses and a headdress. He then checked the name on the pass, which read "Abu Nidal." Now completely satisfied, he said, "All right sir! In you go. . . ."

It still seems possible that compulsory identity cards will be the response to the heightened state of world tension—because the great thing about ID cards is, of course, that they will prevent terrorism. Yup, after years of plotting, encrypted messages, international coordination, secret training, and smuggling weapons, the terrorists will be asked for their ID cards and they'll go, "Drat! Foiled at the last minute! All those years of planning and I forgot to forge an identity card!"

ID cards would naturally represent an outrageous infringement of basic human rights, because they'd mean regularly presenting strangers with a deeply embarrassing photo of yourself. And to make sure the authorities recognised you from the picture, you'd feel the need to pull the same gawky expression that was momentarily caught in the photo booth at the amusement park. Perhaps to set an example politicians should agree that their own identity cards should feature excruciating pictures of themselves from their younger days. A long-haired Tony Blair with huge round collars and sideburns; Jesse Jackson with a big Afro haircut and gold medallions; a young drunken student Dubya mooning the camera.

Whether it means the end of historic freedoms cherished since the Magna Carta I somehow doubt, but I'm against ID cards for other reasons. They've got all the information they want about us already; the trouble is that most of it is wrong. There's probably a computer database somewhere that thinks that "Mr. Duke Edinburgh of Buckingham Place, London" might be interested in subscribing to the *Reader's Digest* Prize Draw. The real oppression of identity cards would not be some Orwellian surveillance nightmare—it will be the more mundane tyranny of having to endure yet another crappy piece of technology that doesn't work properly.

Imagine what fun students will have by drawing an extra couple of lines on each other's bar codes. "I'm afraid, young man, you are not entitled to a student discount because according to this scanner you are a Muller twin-pot yoghurt."

"No, I am a student, really, ask my friend here."

"Well there's no point in talking to him, he's a small tin of Pokémon Pasta Shapes."

Those in favour of ID cards talk in glowing terms about the wonders of modern technology. Identity cards would do more than just prove who you are. All the information that can possibly be needed about you could be stored on one handy smart card replacing all the others in your wallet. A quick swipe will establish that you are prepared to donate your kidneys in the event of an accident, that you

are due a free cappuccino at Caffe Nero, and that eleven months ago
you paid a lot of money to join the local gym but have been there
only twice.

But then police officers will be able to swipe the cards through their
machines and say, "Look Sarge, we've got him now. It says here that
Barney's Big Adventure was due back at Blockbuster Video yesterday
before 11 P.M."

"Oh yeah—and look at this—2,000 accumulated air miles. Been
doing a lot of flying recently, haven't we, sonny?"

Because there is of course a civil liberties issue. As a middle-class
white male I don't suffer much aggravation from the police. Whenever my car is pulled over, I utter a few words and they are suddenly
very polite.

"Is this your own accent, sir?"

"Yes it is."

"That's fine sir, thank you, we're just doing a random check of
accents in the area. Sorry to have troubled you."

But for young black men, failure to produce an identity card on
demand could be used as a reason for further harassment. Asylum
seekers, stigmatised enough already, will be made to feel even more
like nonpersons without official ID cards.

The opposition should not be so obvious as to come out against
ID cards altogether. Instead they should insist that the processing is
done by the people at the IRS. That should hold things up for the
next couple of decades. And then just when they're getting on top
of it, all the politicians could send in their own forms. That'll really
put a spanner in the works.

"Oh no, the members of Parliament have just blown the whole
ID cards scheme out of the water." "How come?" "We should have
thought of this. They've got no identities to put on the cards."

TIME TO LOOSEN
OUR BELTS

20 October 2001

L ast week I was in a pub with some friends and after a couple of pints of beer realised I ought to be heading home. But then I thought about how tourism has been damaged by the events of 9/11, how the recession is starting to affect the leisure and catering sectors, and I thought, "No—by not spending any more money in this pub I'd be doing exactly what those extremists wanted." So I resolved to defy terrorism and have another pint. In fact I defied terrorism several more times after that, and then we all defied terrorism some more by going for Chinese and eventually sharing a taxi home. It was expensive and time-consuming but these are the sorts of sacrifices we should all be prepared to make in times of national crisis.

In the United States, Weight Watchers has reported significant weight gains among its members as patriotic U.S. citizens do their utmost to help the economy by trying every single pudding on the dessert trolley. Some analysts have attributed the increase to a renewed sense of perspective and a grim fatalism that makes counting calories seem irrelevant. But the reality is that people are always looking for an excuse to have whatever they want and if September 11 is the nearest justification at hand then that'll do fine. In World War II people could not help but lose weight, but as we slide into the sequel, Mayor Giuliani is calling for more people to go to restaurants. It's time to loosen our belts. With a recession looming it has become our patriotic duty to spend as much as we can on consumer goods, and Tony Blair has been leading the way as he flies around the Middle East.

"President Musharraf, the British prime minister just called. He's coming to see you again and asked if you wanted him to pick up any more duty-free at the airport."

"Oh yes, 200 Marlboro Lights please."

"Oh but no more ciggies—he's used up his allocation getting a load of B&H for Sheik Zayed of Oman. How about a big Toblerone?"

Indeed it's only Tony Blair's shuttle diplomacy that's keeping the airline companies afloat at the moment. Too many people remain anxious about flying, which is quite ridiculous. Statistics show that you are still far more likely to die at home following a terrorist chemical weapon attack. You've got less chance of being killed in a plane than you have of being wiped out by the anthrax virus, so there's really nothing to worry about.

Bin Laden wanted this recession, so now we must all contribute to the war against terrorism by buying loads of stuff we don't need. "Once more on to the shopping mall, dear friends, once more!" Carpet manufacturers would like us to do our bit by buying more carpets. Or maybe we could stand shoulder to shoulder with our American allies by having a conservatory built onto the back of the house. If there is any capital outlay that you've been putting off, now's the time for getting yourself into debt and splashing out. "That's one in the eye for the al Qaeda network," you can say to yourself as you unpack your new DVD player with surround-sound.

But although we must spend more, it is also our duty to expect less in our wage packet. One business group last month called for a cut in the minimum wage in order to stave off recession. And can you believe it, the unions were against this idea! How can these lefties be so insensitive at this hour to break the prevailing sense of peace and unity by opposing this patriotic suggestion from our company directors? You'd think low-paid workers would be delighted to do their bit by slipping back below the poverty line but no, even after all the suffering that we have seen, they are selfishly clinging onto their £4.10 an hour. Okay, so the recession started before September 11, but anyone who claims it's the fault of anyone except bin Laden must be on his side.

The businessmen who try to use the current crisis to increase their profits are the corporate equivalent of those bereaved relatives who rush back from granny's funeral to be first to grab all the silver. "It's what she would have wanted," they say as they flog off her best stuff at the car boot sale. In America, this syndrome has been dubbed "hitchhiking": major corporations have been using the September 11 tragedy as an argument for lifting restrictions that were placed on them by previous Democratic administrations. "I think as a mark of respect we should be allowed to drill for oil in the National Park," or "In order to send out a clear message about freedom we are asking for federal health and safety regulations to be abolished." "Business as usual" was the slogan that appeared outside bombed corner shops in the last war. "Big business even more appalling than usual" is the axiom of this one.

HOW DO YOU SOLVE THE
PROBLEM OF OSAMA?

27 October 2001

On September 11, soon after two jets were crashed into the World Trade Center causing the twin towers to collapse to the ground, an Internet poll was set up by one of America's leading search engines. It said, "This time have the terrorists gone too far?" Hmmm— a tricky one to call, but apparently most people voted "Yes." Perhaps this was an elaborate surveillance scam by the CIA. They were waiting for someone to click on the little "No" button, and then the marines could dash round in the hope that they'd finally located Osama bin Laden.

In fact the reality is not that different. This week the Pentagon publicly appealed for help in "defeating difficult targets"—announcing a competition for ordinary Americans to come up with snappy ideas on ways of thwarting the terrorists. "We're open to ideas from just about everybody," said Pentagon spokesman Glenn Flood as the guys in the mail room went "Oh terrific; another million strangely addressed envelopes to check out."

So far the only entrant to this competition is a man called G. W. Bush from Washington whose idea was to blow up the whole of Afghanistan. To be fair to the U.S. military, they're doing their best to give due consideration to Afghan civilians. All the American planes have little stickers on the back saying "How's my bombing?" and then there's a number that you can call if you think the U.S. Air Force is blowing up any cities in a discourteous or aggressive manner. Despite this, a great deal of damage has apparently still been done and Kabul's chances of bidding for the next Olympic Games now look like a long shot.

It doesn't exactly fill you with confidence that the moment the world's only superpower is faced with a military foe, they call a press conference and say to the world's media, "Er—I don't suppose you guys have any ideas, do you?" In 1940 when France had fallen and Churchill broadcast to the nation to stiffen British resolve he didn't say, "Er—well frankly we're a bit stuck about what to do at this end, so we thought we'd have a little competition. Answers on a postcard please, send your entries to 'Defeat the Nazis competition, Ministry of War, Whitehall,' and remember the lucky winner gets some book tokens and a seat at the Yalta conference to help decide the postwar settlement."

Washington is so desperate for ideas that they have said that the contest is open to anyone and that the winner could be offered a Pentagon contract. The trouble is that there are housewives in the Midlands who make a living out of repeatedly winning competitions from *Take a Break* magazine and the back of cereal packets; they're bound to have a head start on the rest of us. When the invasion of Kabul goes horribly wrong we'll find out that this is because the assault was planned by a retired dinner lady from Birmingham.

There's already been a setback when the U.S. military found that its precision bombing was not quite as accurate as had been hoped. When the White House announced that they'd be using their famous smart bombs in Afghanistan, workers rebuilding the Chinese embassy in Belgrade three thousand miles away said "Oh no—but we'd nearly finished it" before dashing off to the bomb shelter. So then the Pentagon had the idea of dropping food supplies to the victims of the Taliban. The logic being that if these were aimed really carefully at the fleeing refugees they would miss so comprehensively that you could be sure they'd land right on top of Osama bin Laden, instantly crushing him to death. Okay, so it's an outside chance, but the competition has been going only a few days.

SNAKES AND PROPERTY LADDERS

4 November 2001

When a great public building becomes vacant, the planning people must sit around for hours and hours thinking what on earth it could possibly be used for. "I don't know maybe this is a bit crazy and shoot me down if I'm way off beam here, but how about . . . luxury flats?"

A stunned silence falls around the room at the incredible originality of this idea, the sheer audacity of such lateral thinking.

"What do you mean, convert an old Victorian building originally intended for public use into small luxury domestic units to sell to young professionals? It couldn't be done, could it?"

Meanwhile the yuppies already living in the area are appalled at what is happening. "Look Rupert, they're converting the old children's hospital into 125 maisonettes." "That's terrible. Why only 125?"

The demand for yuppie flats cannot be infinite; surely sooner or later they must run out of yuppies. What will they do then, start converting all the properties back again? "Ya, we got rid of the extra TV room at the top of the house and had it converted back into a traditional attic. It cost a fortune but we covered up the skylight, put in a rusty water tank and rolls of pink insulation felt, and then filled it all up with kindergarten collages, Mother's wedding dress, and broken Christmas tree lights."

Many people feel compelled to buy because of the social stigma that has become attached to renting. In most European cities renting remains a sensible and respectable option but ever since Mrs. Thatcher went down to Home Depot to buy a new door for 10 Downing Street, anyone who does not own their home is now looked down on. I blame all those magazine features in which minor celebrities describe "A Room of My Own." Why can't the Sunday papers feature ordinary people in "A Room of My Landlord's"? Scruffy students could then be photographed slumped in dingy studio apartments, describing how the swirly brown carpet was chosen to match the brown stains on the walls. "Of course this sofa is genuine nylon . . ." says Degsy from his apartment overlooking the railway lines. "And I'm particularly fond of this dangerously wired water heater. . . . I keep it in the hope that it might electrocute some of the silverfish that live in the cutlery drawer."

I have never understood how our cities continue to function when three-quarters of the accommodation is permanently beyond the reach of most of their residents. And why is it a good thing when house prices go up? "There was a double dose of bad news on the economy today. Inflation was up and to make things even worse house prices are still falling."

It all started to go wrong a long time ago, right back when *Homo sapiens* started to shelter in caves. The supply of caverns was limited and prices started to rocket. Neanderthal real estate agents would show prospective buyers around trying to talk up the cave's best points.

"What about heating; what's that like?"

"I know it feels a little chilly at the moment but that's because we're in the middle of an ice age. But it's not a smoke-free zone or anything so you'd be able to have a real fire just as soon as man discovers it."

"Great! And the current occupier will definitely move out on completion, won't he?"

"What, about the sabre-toothed tiger? Um, definitely, yup, no problem there; just tell him you're the new cave owner and he'll be only too happy to move on, I'm sure. . . ."

Then primitive hunter-gatherers turned to agriculture and built the first farmhouses, soon adding a couple of spare rooms to let out for bed and breakfast for weekend visitors. Eventually the Industrial Revolution came and everyone moved to the towns, huddled with a few belongings at some rural railway station as the announcer apologized for the delay, but this was because they still hadn't finished building the line to Liverpool.

And today millions of people live their entire lives in cities like London or New York, but to own your own home in such a place involves going through various distressing stages. Phase one is the nightmare that is the flat-share. This is the period early in your adult life when you permanently fall out with your friends by living with them. The only way to get the British government to understand the seriousness of London's housing crisis would be to force the cabinet to flat-share themselves. They should all have to live together in a poky five-bedroom house in the East End.

"All right . . ." says Tony, opening the fridge in the morning. "Who's been eating my guacamole?" "Your what?" says his working-class deputy, sitting there in his vest reading the tabloids. "I thought those mushy peas tasted a bit funny. Oh by the way, Gordon—you owe me three quid for the milk bill."

"What!" explodes the finance minister. "Look, just because we have seven thousand pounds in the food kitty, that does not mean we can afford to go off buying luxuries like food. And Mo, do you mind not smoking your herbal cigarettes at the breakfast table? And why does she keep giggling at the family on the cornflakes packet?"

Eventually flat-sharers separate off into couples and lock themselves into their bedrooms to bitch about the others. At this point the "luckier" ones scrape together a tiny deposit to buy a rabbit hutch in the outer suburbs. Even a tiny two-bedroom leasehold rabbit hutch without a little glass water dispenser will still set them back £150,000. (When rabbits have dinner parties, it's all they talk about. "My owners looked at a two-bedroom hutch in Kensington; it was £350,000 and that was without straw." "I know it's ridiculous; we were hoping to start a family on Wednesday but we're going to have to wait until the weekend at least." Many central London pets are now having to rent one- room hutches way out in the Thames Estuary and then commute in every morning on the Underground. And once those hamsters start running the wrong way up the down escalator you just can't get them off it.)

Figures released this week show the biggest leap in dinner party conversations about house prices for five years. Discussions about the cost of a three-bedroom semi were up 5 percent from last year, while smug anecdotes about how little couples paid for their own home a few years back are up a massive 17 percent.

"My family only paid a pound for this place and now it's worth a hundred million."

"Yes, but you are the Queen, Ma'am."

Eventually the new homeowners feel compelled to try to buy a larger family house with a separate bedroom for the kids, but such is the financial burden that one of the parents ends up spending the entire night at the office anyway. Journalists in the third world write moving accounts of how Westerners are sold into slavery by taking out their fifth mortgage. "These poor English families remain bonded in debt to the banks for the rest of their lives. Despite working from

morning till night they are told that their debt is actually larger than
it was when they originally took out the loan." The reason that so
many homeowners are struggling to get into the game of snakes and
property ladders is the exorbitant profits made by the mortgage companies. Imagine if a dodgy-looking bloke in a sheepskin coat with two
hard men lurking behind him knocked on your door and offered you
a loan. "I'll lend you a hundred grand. You pay me back one hundred
and seventy grand. But don't forget to pay, because we'd hate to see
you lose your house, wouldn't we boys?"

"Well it's a big profit, but I suppose you have to cover your
expenses."

"Ah yes, the survey fee, that's another £500 you owe us."

"Oh well, I suppose you've got all your paperwork . . ."

"Good point, that's another grand for our 'arrangement fee.'"

"Blimey, well I suppose you have to think of the risks . . ."

"Which is why you'll also be taking out my insurance policy—tell
him, Ron. . . ."

You'd rightly think they were con men. But those are exactly the
sort of mortgage figures you'd be quoted by the banks today. At least
when Brazilian bandits drug you and steal one of your kidneys they
don't charge you for the operation.

The spiralling property market is a symptom of the widening gap
between rich and poor. With too many people earning more than
they can possibly spend, they are buying flats to let out or little weekend cottages in the Isle of Wight. Now when it's closing time on
Friday night in the pubs of West London, the landlord shouts, "Come
on, haven't you got second homes to go to?" We have a property crisis because the rich are too rich. But you can't blame them for wanting to get out of the inner cities on the weekend. I mean London
can be so ghastly sometimes, what with all those homeless people on
the streets and everything.

In order to keep properties at the sort of prices where ordinary people can afford to buy, I think each of us has a duty to lower the tone of our neighbourhoods. If you see a real estate agent showing a posh couple a house on your road, wander out onto the pavement wearing only your pants and polythene raincoat and offer them a taste of one of your homemade bovine spine-burgers. "Hello, are you thinking of buying the old Used Needles Recycling Center? Apparently the garden's still full of them." They'll try to drive away as fast as they can, until they discover that the neighbours on the other side have already stacked their car up on bricks and nicked all the wheels.

We have to do something to bring down house prices because the alternative will be cities in which the demand for cardboard boxes in shop doorways will grow so overwhelming that realtors will end up featuring them in their windows. "Compact, bijou starter home, close to shops. Well, in the doorway, to be honest." And for the average twenty-something, the property pages of the local paper will be more valuable than ever. Not to find a home that they can still afford, but as blankets for when they've given up even trying.

FUNDAMENTALLY
ANTI-FAITH SCHOOLS

17 November 2001

The hills are alive with the sound of music! Like Baron Von Trapp, the Taliban had banned all singing, but now Julie Andrews (in the guise of the Northern Alliance backed up by B-52s) has brought the sound of music back to the hills of Afghanistan. Now in Kabul's West End they are singing the old tunes once more. "I Have Confidence in George Bush"; "Bomb Every Mountain"; and "How Do You Solve the Problem of Osama?"

Even the greatest cynics and antiwar campaigners should celebrate the fall of the most hated tyrants since the advent of car clamping. Suddenly thousands of Afghan children are now experiencing the joy of flying kites once more. And then two minutes later saying, "Actually, this is quite boring. You haven't got a Playstation 2 by any chance, have you?"

The Taliban was a regime made up of former religious students. Afghanistan is what happens when you hand the government over to those kids at school who actually wanted to do Religious Education. And yet in Britain we are increasing the role of religion in our schools. As church and state are being separated in Kabul, we are proposing that the next generation of Britons be educated in a more religious environment. Let us be in no doubt of the terrible fate that lies at the end of the faith schools road. The Middle East will come to Middle England; militant Christians will seize power in a religious revolution that will see Britain become the first-ever fundamentalist Christian state (or second after Alabama).

After declaring the Archbishop of Canterbury the new head of state, the religious students will impose an austere regime based on the harsh strictures of their own extreme brand of English Christianity. Women will be forced to observe a strict dress code and made to wear long floral dresses with puffy sleeves. Men will wear Aran sweaters and sandals and be too cheerful. A Christian mob clutching tambourines and chanting "Kumbaya" will surround the supermarkets, forcing them to close their doors on the sabbath. The only shopping permitted on Sunday will be at the bring-and-buy sale at the vicarage where the local populace will be coerced into purchasing little spider plants and homemade jam. Where Afghan kids shouted "Allah is great!" English schoolchildren will chant the central tenet of Church of England doctrine: "There probably is a god, though perhaps not in the literal sense, more as a sort of spiritual concept maybe." There will be no music except Christian rock, so there will be no music. An exception will be made for the singing of hymns; it will be compulsory for everyone to go to church and self-consciously mumble their way through the second verse of "To Be a Pilgrim," and then sing out the last line loud and clear to make up for not knowing the rest of it. It will be an offence to get out of bed in the morning only because "Thought for the Day" has just come on the radio. School nativity plays will not be permitted to edit the original biblical text and so will go on for several days. Loose adaptations will also be forbidden, so having the Virgin Mary clutching a plastic Baby Annabel from Toys 'R' Us and then singing Spice Girls hits is definitely out. Anyone breaking any of these strict Christian laws will face instant forgiveness.

Of course all this is a ridiculous fantasy. Nothing so foolish could ever come to pass. Future schoolchildren will learn about the dawn of a lasting world peace when they study this period of history in their new faith schools. For what could be more conducive to world peace than having all the Christian kids in one school and all the Muslim kids in a different school down the road? Why not stick a Jewish school in the middle and have an interschools jihad on sports day?

Creating new faith schools now seems about as sensible as a Taliban version of *Pop Idol*. "Well, we don't know what she looks like and we're not allowed to hear her sing so we'll just have to hope for the best." You'd think the government would have enough problems on its hands deciding what to do with all these Taliban leaders, without setting up new faith schools back home that'll be needing religious heads to run them all. Oh no, they wouldn't, would they? Suddenly it all fits together. . . .

OSAMA'S CHRISTMAS MESSAGE

29 December 2001

Well, by now we have all seen that infamous video message and listened to all the experts analysing every detail: those staring eyes, the gray hair, the lined face, that religious fervour. But still the question remains: what was the Queen's Christmas message designed to achieve? Many experts believe that the address may have actually been recorded some time ago at one of her secret hideouts—possibly in the mountains surrounding Balmoral. But why did she choose to release her Christmas message over the Christmas period? Perhaps the recording was an attempt to prove that she is still alive, or perhaps a coded message to her supporters. But why did she not move her left hand? Was it tired from a whole year of waving?

Sadly any attempt by the Queen to get her message across was completely upstaged by another millionaire religious leader—Osama bin Laden. This Christmas the Arabic satellite news channel Al-Jazeera pipped the BBC to top the holiday ratings with their Osama bin Laden Christmas special. What is amazing is that bin Laden managed to talk for thirty-three minutes (or an hour once the Americans had put in the commercial breaks) without managing to answer any of the questions that the West is desperate to know. Where is he hiding? What is he planning next? Why doesn't "Al Qaeda" have a letter "u" after the "q"? And how is it that a parcel containing the video sent from Pakistan a week ago can arrive more quickly than a Christmas card sent a couple of miles across London? In fact, the video really tells us only one thing: Osama got a camcorder for Christmas. (The FBI are questioning Sony to see if he sent back his guarantee card.) Now bin Laden's made a video of himself, which is exactly the sort of cry for attention you'd expect from the middle child from a family of fifty-four children. Next week the offices of *America's Funniest Home Videos* will receive a tape of a contrived "accident" of Osama walking past a swimming pool and falling in fully clothed as the Al Qaeda network desperately tries to raise a bit more cash. The delay between the tape's recording and transmission is easily explained. Imagine the scene in the cave: "Right, we have made the recording, Osama. Now to transfer it onto this videotape." "No not that one—I just recorded 'The Simpsons Christmas Special' on that one." "Oh all right, what about this one?" "No—that's got *Ally McBeal* on it." "Oh come on—you're never going to watch that now." "I am, I am, look, what's on this one? Honestly why can't you label your bloody videos?" "Um, I think that's *Before They Were Famous*. I wanted to see if they've dug up that clip of Osama on *Ed McMahon's Star Search*."

In his video address bin Laden discusses the American action in Afghanistan, although his exact words depend on whose translation you read. For example the Pentagon version has him saying, "I now see that American foreign policy is totally benign and justified, oh yes. The United States is truly a wonderful country and I never miss *West Wing* or *Sex and the City*, oooh I really fancy a McDonald's cheeseburger and vanilla shake and no mistake." If you put this version to one side, there was very little in the half-hour monologue of any great surprise. He reads a poem and his eyes go all watery but frankly it's just all too static, too much "talking heads." The producers of David Letterman used to get round this problem by putting in some stupid pet tricks. Or maybe Osama should have put in some sketches to break it up a bit; either way his style is too wooden and the content too thin for this unsolicited pilot to get its own series. So a letter has gone back to the Tora Bora mountains thanking Osama for his tape but explaining that the BBC gets a lot of videos from people wanting to be on television but competition is extremely fierce, etc., although his details have been sent to Independent Television for its new series called *Celebrity Cave Makeover*. Filming starts as soon as the location manager finds it.

TYSON BITES YER LEGS

26 January 2002

M ike Tyson said in his defence this week that he is not Mr. Politically Correct. Self-knowledge is a wonderful thing. I'd say the convicted rapist who once assaulted elderly car drivers in a road rage incident, attacked journalists and photographers, spends much of his time in hostess bars making obscene crotch-grabbing gestures, and is wanted on further sexual charges is indeed probably a bit of a long shot for the post of professor of gender studies at Vassar College.

Yet Mike Tyson remains a role model for thousands. Where I live in South London far more young working-class men have named their pet Rottweilers "Tyson" than, say, "Chomsky." You never see these blokes standing in the park shouting "Yoko, come here!" or "de Beauvoir! Get down!"

But this week their hero sank to another new low. In a staged press conference with Lennox Lewis, he proved unable to wait until the fight proper and attacked Lewis after just ten seconds, even biting his intended opponent in the foot. The event was designed to generate publicity but it was far too successful.

Mike Tyson is supposed to be on medication to control his temper. They said to him, "Mike, you know you're a professional boxer—well we're giving you these drugs to stop you being so aggressive." No wonder he's so cross. The visits to the doctor were always a tense affair; last time his physician gave him a gentle tap on the knee with a little rubber hammer. That doctor gets out of the hospital sometime next month.

Tyson became world heavyweight at the age of twenty back in 1986. But things started to go wrong fairly quickly. Soon afterward he was knocked unconscious when he crashed his car into a tree, with the result that for a brief period the WBO heavyweight title was held by a large horse chestnut. The tree then bought lots of gold jewellery and was photographed dating Miss Wyoming and pretty soon, well, he just went to seed. Tyson regained the world title, but has since been to prison, been fined for punching a referee, and been banned for biting off an opponent's ear. Still it's better than bottling it all up. Onlookers were particularly shocked when they saw him spit out Holyfield's ear. He could have at least popped it discreetly into a little napkin.

Tyson's behaviour only gives ammunition to those who would have the sport of boxing banned altogether. I can understand why some consider the sport to be barbaric, but these are often people who have had more career choices than those upon whom they would sit in judgment. When I was a young boy growing up in my pretty riverside village, boxing was the only way out of the middle-class ghetto. It was either boxing or accountancy. Okay, boxing, accountancy, law, medicine, investment banking, journalism, business consultancy, or becoming a database developer for one of the emerging software companies springing up all along the Silicon Valley. Maybe Tyson should redirect his energies toward a sport less likely to bring out his violent side. Figure skating, for example, or synchronised swimming.

Because this week's ugly scenes probably won't be the last, and every time the moral commentators become even more outraged; why, these boxers—they are behaving in a violent and aggressive manner! If the boxing authorities had the long-term interests of boxing at heart, they would have nothing more to do with Mike Tyson. It would mean resisting the immediate prize of a huge multimillion-dollar fight, of course, so that's obviously going to happen. In fact Tyson's notoriety only helps generate more interest and put up his price. I don't know, maybe I'm being a bit cynical here, but it's almost as if somebody somewhere is more interested in the money than the sport. No, that's probably unfair, I take that back completely.

AS ENGLISH AS
BASEBALL ITSELF

9 February 2002

Yesterday's proposed bill on immigration and citizenship proposed that immigrants to the United Kingdom swear an oath of allegiance to the Queen and demonstrate an ability to speak English that would have ruled out most of her ancestors. The full text of the pledge requires new arrivals to uphold British values and democratic traditions—so from now on they'll stop bothering to vote at elections and will just moan about everything instead.

Some immigrants to England do seem to have slightly naïve ideas about what life in Britain is like. Anyone who tries to get into the UK by clinging to the underneath of a train should have it politely explained to them that in the UK the trains don't actually go any-where. But if there is going to be a test for British citizenship, it should at least reflect the reality of the British character. For a start, in the line for applications, if anyone is seen twitching nervously in case that man hovering near the front was thinking of pushing in, they should get extra "British-ness" points straight away. However, when someone does barge to the front of the line the ideal applicant should whisper to her husband, "I'm going to say something," to which he should reply, "Shh dear, best not make a fuss," and that couple will have then passed stage one with flying colours. Then comes the tough written test, and anyone who completes this without a single grammatical error or spelling mistake will be told to go straight back to Holland.

Question 1: Please list the following events in order of historical importance. (a) The French Revolution. (b) The end of the Cold War. (c) *Chariots of Fire* winning the 1982 Oscar for Best Picture. Question 2: What is the traditional accompaniment to spaghetti bolognese? (a) a light sprinkling of grated parmesan cheese or (b) a large portion of chips and two slices of white bread. Question 3: A man trips on the pavement and bumps into you. Do you (a) cast him a slightly annoyed look and continue on your way or (b) say, "Oh I'm terribly sorry, really; my fault entirely. . . ."

Immigration to Britain is nothing new, although in the old days the speed at which applications were processed often depended on how big your army was. Back in 1066, for example, the small immigration office at Hastings was completely overwhelmed: "Right sir, while your army is filling out form 7R(B)—*Application for Admission to Wessex by non-Saxon Residents*—can I just ask you the purpose of your visit to the UK?"

"Well, to overthrow the incumbent Saxon monarchy, install a brutal regime based on fear and murder, and seize all wealth and property for myself and my fellow Normans."

"Fine, just as long as you weren't planning to take on any paid employment while you were here. . . ."

At which point one of the lancers had to go home because he'd been hoping to do a little bit of bar work.

Today we hope to make assimilation a more peaceful process. The government wants immigrants to become fully integrated into British society and obviously the best way to do this is to have all the Muslims go to one school and have all the Christians attend another one down the road. But the home secretary's draft bill has now been upstaged by his comments about arranged marriages. He suggested that it would be better for people to choose their marriage partners from here in Britain rather than from Asia, which greatly upset some fat old white men who were looking at a website based in Thailand. Of course for most Britons it has not been customary for our parents to arrange our marriages. Instead we have both sets of in-laws come to stay at Christmas and there then follows an arranged divorce.

When politicians talk about race, and indeed religion, every single care must be taken, not just because it is so easy to give offence, but because there are racists in our society who need only the slightest misheard cue to justify racial violence. Which makes it all the more ironic that the home secretary had to back down when he attempted to outlaw the incitement of religious hatred. Some people tried to claim this would make it illegal to impersonate a vicar, which was clearly ridiculous. What did they think Tony Blair has been doing for the last five years?

WAR! HURR! WHAT IS IT GOOD FOR?

30 March 2002

Twenty years ago this week the news came through that Argentina had invaded the Falkland Islands. Details were sketchy in those first few hours, though some people thought they might be in the Indian Ocean maybe, or perhaps near Australia somewhere. While the Foreign Office was still leafing through its big dusty atlas with the British Empire bits coloured in pink, Margaret Thatcher had already decided to go to war. Almost overnight she went from being a vulnerable and deeply unpopular prime minister to being an unassailable politician who was then in a position to do to British industry what she'd just done to the Argentine navy. A fascist dictatorship was toppled in Argentina, but apart from that, everything went the way she wanted it.

Now in the same way George W. Bush has been turned from discredited leader to popular national hero by embarking on military action overseas. They are rewriting the lyrics to Edwin Starr's classic peace anthem. Now it goes, "War! Hurr! What is it good for? Approval ratings for national leaders, yeah! War! Hurr! What is it good for? Deflecting attention from complex domestic problems! Say it again!"

Back in 1982 America supported Britain in the Falklands War on condition that the British government sign a special contract drawn up by the Pentagon, which stated, "In return for U.S. backing, Britain hereby promises to support every armed intervention that America undertakes forever and ever, and to take endless reruns of *Barney and Friends*." There can't be any other explanation for Britain's consistent enthusiasm for every American bombing raid or new missile deployment. When the White House declared a war on drugs, British jets were scrambled ready to bomb a solitary dope dealer in downtown Detroit. If the president's daughter reveals her battle with underage drinking, then British commandos are sent into battle with the demon drink on her behalf.

But if we believe we can influence U.S. foreign policy by sticking beside America then we are deluding ourselves. Britain can no more affect the direction being taken than some teenage girl gripping onto the passenger seat as her joyriding boyfriend speeds out of control.

One day in the not too distant future, Tony Blair will appear in tears opposite George W. Bush on the Jerry Springer show. "On today's programme, 'World leaders who promised special relationships.'" The host will put a reassuring hand on the British PM's shoulder as a bitter Tony recounts how much he did for this guy: he went to war for him, he stuck up for him when no one else would, even though all his friends warned him not to get too close. Because George had promised Tony that they would always do everything together. But then bang! bang! and it was all over; George had got what he wanted and he wasn't bothered about Tony anymore. And then the audience will boo George from Texas as he shrugs and sneers, "Hey, I get into bed with whoever suits me—who knows what I promised Terry here." Cue the shouting and the undignified scuffle as they cut to the ads and Jerry Springer says, "Coming up after these messages: 'My brother screwed Florida!'"

In the hysteria of the moment all wars can seem justifiable. When the War of Jenkins' Ear broke out in 1739, all the woolly liberals were going around saying, "Well, this Jenkins chap did have his ear chopped off after all, so I think an all-out war against Spain is the only justifiable course of action." But if the invasion of Iraq is such a great idea, why weren't we lobbying America to pursue this policy before they told us about it when they faxed through the infantry request form? We would all love to see Saddam Hussein being overthrown but this has to be brought about by the people of Iraq. There are plenty of appalling regimes around the world and some we arm and some we bomb. In Saddam's case we have done both just to be on the safe side. If ever Arab support for peace in the Middle East needs to be courted it is now. So what does the American president think? "I know! Why don't we invade Iraq? Because things are so quiet between Israel and the Palestinians at the moment that a U.S. bombing of an Arab state would probably go down really well." Tony Blair has to put some distance between himself and the Global Village Idiot. The Labour party might be able to forgive its leader for behaving like a president, but they could never forgive him for behaving like *that* president.

And then Tony Blair should explain to Bush that Britain can go to war only in extreme circumstances and when very precise criteria have been met. "I'm sorry, George, but Britain can bomb or invade a country only where the leader has not been democratically elected and where the regime has recently executed British citizens. Oh no, hang on, that's America, isn't it? I think we'd better think this out again. . . ."

DOES THE WORKING
CLASS EXIST?

13 April 2002

This week a writ was submitted to the High Court that stated, "The words 'working classes' are not now capable of any meaningful definition." The judge looked up from his tabloid newspaper, took a stubby pencil from behind his ear, and said, "Ooh dear, nah mate, a court case like that's gonna cost yer, innit? And we're booked up for ages—tell you what, I'll see if one of me mates can adjudicate for yer, I'll just get me mobile from the van."

The assertion that the working classes no longer exist is being made by a property company that wants to develop a site in central London for luxury housing despite a 1929 covenant that states that the land may be used only to provide housing for the working classes. The clause goes on to say that they must have tattoos, have a car stacked up on bricks in the front garden, and always eat dinner in front of the television.

The original 1929 clause was clearly intended to safeguard housing for ordinary people doing low-paid jobs, and today this need is greater than ever. Obviously the working classes are not the same as they were in the 1920s. They're not all wearing flat caps and saying to a wobbly black-and-white camera, "Well I'm just a simple working

man and don't know nuffink about no gold standard but if that
Mr. Churchill says we's ought go back on it, well that's good enuff
for the likes of me!"

To hear some of the commentators on this story over the past
couple of days you would think they'd never met a working-class
person in their lives. (Presumably their cleaners are from the Philip-
pines so that doesn't count.) It's like we're talking about some nearly
extinct species that could be tracked down only after days spent trek-
king through the urban jungle. You can almost imagine the next
nature documentary from the BBC, featuring a memorable piece of
footage in which a naturalist encounters a surviving family group of
the endangered species known as "working-class people." He whis-
pers to the camera that he is going to try to get closer. At first they
are wary of him; the dominant male grunts and furrows his eyebrows
before returning to feed on his natural diet of Doritos and Tang. The
mother seems anxious about her new offspring; he's still not back from
the shop with her ciggies, but the older cubs are more playful, and
before long are climbing all over David Attenborough and nicking
his mobile phone.

In the old days you could tell what social class people belonged to
by their size: the rich people were fat and the poor people were thin.
Apparently the poor didn't eat much and had to walk everywhere,
in direct contrast to today of course, where Homer Simpson lies
around all day in front of the telly eating pork rinds while the high
earners are starving themselves on a lettuce leaf and spending an hour
a day on a Stairmaster. But there are also all sorts of ways in which
the classes overlap. I might decide to get myself a proletarian supper
of fish and chips but then I'll go and give myself away by asking if
the vinegar is balsamic. (I hadn't had such a funny look since I asked
if it was organic free-range chicken in the KFC bargain bucket.)
Ultimately it still comes down to money. The working classes are

embarrassed that they don't have more of it, and the English middle classes are mortified that they have so much. All these determining factors will be gone over in the High Court later this year. My prediction is that the court will rule in favour of the property company, thereby finally establishing in law that the British working classes are indeed finally extinct. In other words the law courts will have sided with the posh chaps from the property company in wealthy Surrey. And what more proof do you need that the English class system is alive and well and still screwing the working classes as much as ever? It makes my middle-class blood boil so much I want to tut and say "honestly!," but best not make a fuss, I suppose.

SUNDAY DADS

28 May 2002

The problem of fathers who don't spend enough time with their families is an issue throughout the animal kingdom. The worker bee, for example, spends all his time out with his mates supping pollen, while the poor queen bee is stuck inside producing around 100,000 eggs a week. No doubt when she was younger she had all these plans about travelling and starting a career, but then one day she had an egg, and then three seconds later she had another one, and suddenly she found herself trapped in the hive, feeling fat and fed up and stuffing her face with royal jelly all day.

After billions of years of evolution, however, *Homo sapiens* has finally reached the stage where the male is occasionally prepared to get more involved in the care of the little ones. Some of the more advanced men relish this opportunity but for most it is something they do reluctantly and as infrequently as possible. This subspecies is known as the Sunday Dad. He spends time with his kids once a week, and according to my wife, even then he has an ulterior motive. "Typical male!" she says. "He's only looking after them to get out of clearing up after lunch."

You see these Sunday Dads looking lost in public parks, pushing the baby's buggy with only one hand to give the impression that it's not actually theirs, that they're just looking after it for someone. Just as less socially aware dog owners pretend not to notice when the Great Dane on the end of their lead leaves a pile of dog mess that can be seen by passing aircraft, the Sunday Dad will try and make out that those noisy children clutching his leg and shouting "Daddy!" are nothing to do with him. Sometimes his determination to ignore his kids reaches heroic proportions. He may be sitting in a ball pit, with his offspring screaming and throwing brightly coloured plastic balls at his head, but he will still give the impression that this is a perfectly normal place for an adult to go and read the Sunday papers. Wherever he is with his children, his mind is somewhere else.

Of course what he's really afraid of is embarrassment. His affected detachment is his way of appearing cool. For if he was to throw himself fully into playing with his kids, the rest of the world might see that he's not actually very good at it. When it came to learning how to deal with the children his wife somehow seemed to have a head start on him. This made it easier to take a back seat and so the gap in their childcare skills grew even wider. At a dinner table he always sat wherever it would be impossible for him to get out when the children needed seeing to. During the night he pretended to be asleep when his wife went to the crying baby for the fourth time. And now he might try to justify all this to himself by imagining that he works very hard; but deep down he knows that it's easier to be rushing about looking important than standing in a freezing cold playground being bored out of your head pushing a swing for the four thousandth time.

It is often the case that the more successful a man is at work, the less use he is in the home. They get so wrapped up in their jobs, they forget to give a second thought to what their wife and children are up to. When Neil Armstrong touched down on the moon, he said to Mission Control, "The Eagle has landed! Oh and Houston, will you call my wife and tell her I won't be home for dinner tonight." Career highfliers who work long hours are also used to getting their own way and having everyone do as they say. But this cuts no ice with his two-year-old and so the Sunday Dad gets a bit of a shock when his toddler lies down on the floor, kicking and screaming and shouting "No!" to every suggestion or demand. Maybe his secretary should try that sometimes.

As they get older the kids soon learn that Dad doesn't really have the faintest idea what they're not allowed, and so he'll find himself coming back from the shops and then getting all defensive with his wife: "Well how was I to know that the kids aren't allowed flamethrowers?" The only other shopping that the Sunday Dad has to do with the kids is choosing a present for Mummy's birthday. Every year he will suddenly realise that he has left it for too late and that the only place left open is the gasoline station. That's when he can be spotted dragging the kids around the Texaco minimart trying to decide if Mummy would prefer a packet of barbecue briquettes, some Castrol GTX, or a polythene-wrapped copy of *Penthouse*.

Sunday Dads are physically absent six days of the week and mentally absent for all seven. But rather than try to change their worker-bee husbands, perhaps their wives ought to look at the example of another insect—the praying mantis. The female of this species has learnt to tackle the problem of the absent male head-on. She chooses the father of her children, mates with him just the once, and then eats him. Apparently this approach goes quite a long way in tempering the resentment that can build up in a marriage. My wife, however, still feels it does not go far enough. "Typical male . . ." she said, "he's not there when it's time to clear up after dinner either."

GOD BLESS THE WORLD CUP

1 June 2002

The Queen has been in a fantastic mood this week. Her golden jubilee appears to have prompted an enormous surge in patriotism, with pubs and cafés all decked out with the English flag.

"But why do all these people celebrating my fifty years on the throne have 'Come On England!' all over their white vans?" she asked her advisors.

"Er, well Ma'am, they are urging the rest of England to 'come on' and celebrate your majesty's jubilee . . ."

"Oh, I see. But why does it say 'Owen Forever'? Isn't he an England footballer?"

"Certainly not, Ma'am, er, that's an acronym. . . . It stands for, erm, Onwards With Elizabeth's Nation . . . yes, that works . . ."

As a simple test of how the English people channel their patriotism, support for the national soccer team has totally eclipsed any interest in the Queen's Golden Jubilee. It's a complete walkover: England Flags 5, Union Jacks 1. (Of course all the flags were actually made in China, but that's another matter.) If the Queen had broken her toe like the England captain two months ago, it's hard to imagine the nation fretting quite so much as to whether she'd have been fit to do royal walkabouts in time for the jubilee bank holiday: "And the news from the Buck House dressing room is that the Queen is looking 50/50 for the royal balcony waving on June 3. The physio laureate has said he doesn't want to push her too fast; some of those red carpets can be pretty treacherous."

It seems logical that the only way for the royal family to increase its popularity would be to adopt some of the trappings of our national sport. Soccer has the advantage of constant television exposure, analysis from a panel of experts, post-match interviews—these are all things that Buckingham Palace needs to think about if they want to force themselves back to the centre of the nation's heart. So after a royal tree planting is replayed for the third time in slow motion, we'll cut straight to the dressing room, where the sports reporter is waiting to talk to a red-faced Prince Charles, as other exuberant royals run behind him, ruffling his sweat-soaked hair.

"So Charles—a very successful tree-planting there. . . . Congratulations!"

"Well, yeah, I didn't know much about it to be honest, the mayor picked up the shovel on my left, he passed it to me, inch-perfect like, and I suddenly saw the base of the tree at my feet and I just buried it!"

Prince Andrew, as president of the Football Association, is currently the only royal directly connected with the beautiful game and last week he flew out for the World Cup's opening ceremony. Apparently there was a terrible delay at the airport when Prince Andrew's name came up on the computer as someone who had a history of travelling abroad with other English lads and getting involved in violence. "Yes, that was the Falklands War, it doesn't count. . . ." he said as he was chucked in the cells with all the tattooed Manchester United fans. Apparently the foul language and obscene singsongs were quite shocking, but the fans soon got used to it.

Andrew's sister remains the only royal to have actually represented her country at the highest level on the sportsfield. In 1972 Princess Anne made the Olympic team for the sport of Poncing Around on a Horse. (The British selectors went on to get the gold medal for sycophantic toadying.) Her Royal Highness jumped all the fences as well as can be expected considering she had a police bodyguard sharing her saddle at all times. Anne's appearance was notable for the bizarre piece of trivia that she was the only competitor at the entire games who was not forced to undergo a sex test. The authorities carefully read through *Debrett's Guide to Etiquette and Modern Manners* and there was absolutely no guidance whatsoever as to how one might tackle the tricky subject of whether a royal princess is actually a fella or not. "The thing is, Your Royal Highness, we do need to be 100 percent sure that you are not actually endowed with a frankfurter as it were, so if you could just quickly lower the old jodhpurs for us, Ma'am, we'll be on our way." A request like this could ruin your chances of being invited to a garden party at Buckingham Palace.

Not until one of the royals actually represents their country in Britain's favourite sport will they be able to claim some sort of stake in their subjects' football-inspired patriotism. Under FIFA rules the Queen could still qualify for this World Cup. Imagine the drama: England in the World Cup final and Her Majesty in goal for the penalty shoot-out. It's just a shame she'd have to play for the Germans.

Until then it would appear that this historic anniversary is being regarded with widespread cynicism and apathy. Unemployed single parents lie around the house saying, "Why should I care about some old woman who happens to be Queen?"

"Because I'm your mother!" she says to them. "Now get off the couch and go and tour Canada or something."

Social commentators are left wondering what has happened to this unpatriotic society when so little respect is shown to our head of state. How different from the happy innocence of her majesty's Silver Jubilee back in 1977, they say. Back then, in village greens across Merrie England, rosy-cheeked teenagers wearing black bin liners and safety pins through their noses spat and pogoed to the sound of the Sex Pistols and the Clash. Yes, the whole nation came together in the unifying spirit of hate and anarchy, the poet laureate Sir John Rotten penned his jubilee poem "God Save the Queen, the fascist regime that made you a moron," and thousands of young citizens with Mohawk haircuts had "No Future" tattooed across their foreheads. Ah, happy days.

In fact the idea that Britain was always a nation of monarch-loving loyalists who spontaneously celebrated every anniversary is about as believable as today's royal wedding vows. Henry III, for example, ruled for fifty-six years but his golden jubilee was a flop. "Henry III?" they said, "Erm, now which one's that then? 'Cos Henry V is Agincourt isn't he, and Henry VIII has six wives and all that, so Henry III—is he the one with the hump who killed the princes in the tower? No, hang on. . . ." Charles I was just approaching his silver jubilee when the committee arranging the festivities decided it might be more fun to chop off his head. And then all the jubilee mugs had to be repainted with just the stump of his neck showing. Other royal celebrations were an even bigger washout; like in 1003 when they asked King Ethelred the Unready if he'd made all the preparations for his street party.

"Oh my god, is that today? I haven't even thought about it yet . . ."

And now in the twenty-first century we are all supposed to dash out into the street, introduce ourselves to the neighbours we've never met before, and organise a spontaneous community knees-up. Street parties are a strange concept. You spend years telling your kids not to step out onto the road, nearly yanking their arms off if they so much as put one foot off the pavement. And then you plonk the kitchen table in the middle of the street and tell them to eat their lunch there.

"What are you crying for, darling?"

"I'm scared! It feels wrong!" stammers the terrified child.

"Don't be silly, now come on, eat up before the table gets clamped!"

(And then the following week her big brother wanders out of McDonald's chomping on a Filet o' Fish and the parents say, "How revolting! Eating your lunch in the middle of the street, honestly dear, can't you eat that indoors?")

Street parties, like the royal family, are just a bit out of fashion. Of course it is not so long since "Palace" was the soap opera of the moment. In the 1980s we had royal weddings, even more royal babies, and Diana and Fergie perfectly reflected the good taste and intellectual rigour of the age. But suddenly the fairy tale went into reverse and the princes turned into toads. Windsor Castle burned down after granny left her vests drying on the paraffin heater and Princess Anne got divorced, prompting a bitter court battle over custody of the horses.

So this year does present us with a wonderful anniversary. It is ten years since the *annus horribilis*, which is not some weird condition you develop from sitting on the throne for too long, but was the Queen's own phrase to describe the year when it all fell apart for the royal family. Nineteen ninety-two was the year the mask slipped and we saw the truth.

So wave that flag and open that champagne. Because for a whole decade now, nobody has cared about the monarchy. Hooray, we won't have to hold a street party and watch our neighbours waiting to race for that parking space right outside their house as soon as the cars are allowed back in the road. In one last-ditch attempt to appear relevant and with it, the monarchists are organising a more modern type of party. Sir Paul McCartney, Mick Jagger, and Sir Elton John are teaming up for a special jubilee pop concert. "Ah! Aren't they marvelous?" the old ladies will say, "the way they just keep on going. They do so much for tourism and they work so hard and you shouldn't criticise them because they can't answer back." Suddenly I agree with all the royalists saying things were better in 1977. It makes you nostalgic for punk. I don't blame the Queen personally, of course, she's just badly advised. No one's advised her to declare a republic.

IN-FLIGHT ENTERTAINMENT

14 June 2002

t's no wonder that Independent TV couldn't get anyone to pay for their various satellite channels. Not when you can watch live footage from U.S. spy planes for free. This week it was revealed that for the past six months it's been possible to watch transmissions from American spy planes with an ordinary satellite dish. What would normally require a secret video link was being broadcast unencrypted across the world via a commercial TV satellite, with a live connection to the Internet just in case one or two terrorists had failed to catch the current U.S. troop movements on their telly.

This bizarre lapse in security was discovered last year, but the broadcasts have still not been halted. If you failed to spot the wacky adventures of the U.S. army listed in your copy of *TV Guide*, don't worry, you can still catch the omnibus edition that goes out on Sunday. If the U.S. military wanted to keep the information top secret they could at least have switched transmission to PBS. If they'd stuck it in the middle of the fund-raising telethon then maybe no one would have ever seen it.

You'd think suspicions would have been raised when the engineer was called out to connect up a new satellite TV package for a Mr. O.

bin Laden at a secret address in the Tora Bora cave complex in the Afghan mountains. "So there's all your movie channels there, you've got Sky Sports, the complete Disney package, and then on channel 71 you've got all the latest movements of U.S. peacekeeping forces in the Balkans."

"Excellent! Now can you tell me when the Shopping Channel is selling anthrax warheads?"

For satellite customers bored of watching reruns of M*A*S*H, the exciting new U.S. spy plane package includes *The Terrorist Channel*, featuring all the latest movements of anti-U.S. terror networks; *Terrorist Kids*, for younger viewers; and *USA Style*, which is a sort of homes and gardens makeover channel. "Okay, let's just remind ourselves how this Afghan village looked before the bombing, and watch the reaction of the red team when they get to see how the U.S. Air Force has managed to completely change the layout of their home in just one hour!" Who wants to watch all that familiar footage from World War II on the Discovery Channel when you can watch all the preparations for World War III being broadcast live twenty-four hours a day?

The spy plane footage could also provide endless outtakes for other programs. Between the home video bloopers of bridesmaids fainting and toddlers getting stuck in their potties, there'll be other endearing human slipups like NATO smart bombs accidentally blowing up the hospital. Instead of watching surveillance footage of speeding joyriders on *America's Worst Car Crashes!* the presenter can tut about the dangerous driving of these irresponsible suicide bombers. "Look at this idiot. If he carries on speeding that lorry load of explosives toward that building, someone could get really hurt!" Ever aware to the possibilities of advertising, it must only be a matter of time before the broadcasters find a suitable sponsor. "And now back to part two of the War on Terrorism, sponsored by Taco Bell." Product placement will mean that instead of chasing terrorists in helicopter gun-ships, U.S. army personnel will be forced to cross mountainous terrain in the latest Subaru Outback. American military operations will be organised into eight-minute slots so that the broadcasters can cut to an ad break at just the right time. Each segment will end with a cliffhanger in case the viewer is tempted to switch channels. "Oh no! The Al Qaeda are about to escape over the border. And I forgot to ring my mom to say happy birthday!"

With so much competition in the new digital TV market, it would seem sensible to include these wonderful new programs in any new package on offer. The expertise demonstrated by the World Cup pundits could be employed at halftime in the latest global sport to hit the airwaves:

"Well frankly, Gary, the Americans are going to have to work a lot harder to close down this Saudi star, bin Laden."

"I couldn't agree more, Terry; I've not been very impressed with the accuracy of these American strikes so far. Here we see the action replay of this attack: look, he completely misses and blows up the Chinese embassy—and at this level you've really got to hit the target."

With coverage like this it won't be long until we are all filling out our War on Terrorism wall chart. And when all-out nuclear warfare does finally break out, at least we'll be able to say to our friends down at the pub, "Don't tell me who wins! I'm taping it and watching it later!"

NO SEX PLEASE,
WE'RE TEENAGE BOYS

29 June 2002

During a recent secondary school production of *The Sound of Music*, a teacher stood up in front of the audience and asked if all mothers with babies in the crèche could come and check if it was their baby that wouldn't stop crying. Half the cast walked off the stage. "I am sixteen, going on seventeen," continued Liesl, with a nine-month bump sticking out of her maternity dress.

The problem of teenage pregnancies is in the news again, with the government announcing that it will be making free condoms available to schoolchildren. In practical terms it is not very clear how these contraceptives will be handed out. Will each class have a condom monitor? Perhaps the boys will be sent down to the chemist to buy them, only to return shamefaced with thirty combs and a toothbrush. Or will the teachers just hand them out at morning registration? "Right, take one and pass the rest back, no don't open them now, Timothy, they are for after school, except for members of sex soc." Or maybe they'll be sold in the school tuck shop (recently wittily renamed by the boys from 4B)? "Er, yeah, can I have a sherbet dib-dab, 100 grams of lemon bonbons, and a super-ribbed featherlite condom please." Seeing who can blow the biggest bubbles will never be the same again.

It is important that teenagers know what these things are for. Now that they're to be made more widely available we can look forward to a dramatic increase in the numbers of condoms being filled up with water and chucked at passersby from the top of the multistorey car park.

Underage sex is not a new problem in Britain. A report back in the seventies showed that boys in their teens were having more sex than ever, although this figure would have dropped dramatically if they'd included me in the survey. Of course these things can be quite difficult to measure. Approaching a class of sixteen-year-old boys and saying, "Right, hands up, who's still a virgin?" may not be the most reliable polling method available. In the developed world, only America actually manages an even higher teenage pregnancy rate than us, and there George Bush is funding an abstinence education programme, telling young people that they should not have sex while every advert, TV show, and movie is telling them the opposite.

It is fashionable on the left to laugh at the idea of abstinence education as misguided and reactionary and if the only thing we were telling our teenagers about sex is "don't do it," then we would obviously fail. But alongside better information, advice, and access to contraception, I would venture that it is a good idea to just add that there is no compulsion for teenagers to lose their virginity quite so early on. Basically what I'm saying is that if I didn't have constant sex as a teenager I don't see why they should.

One way to reduce the pressure on kids to grow up so quickly might be to make sex education more brutally honest about the reality of the adult sexual experience. "Sexual intercourse happens between a man and a woman on Sunday morning. Foreplay traditionally begins with the gentleman being more attentive to his wife than he has been all week, fetching her a second cup of tea, and repeatedly sighing, 'Well, there's nothing worth reading in the Sunday papers!' Three minutes after this the lady says, 'Mmm, that was nice!' and remembers that she'd meant to get up early to deadhead the geraniums." That should put them off the idea for a while. Or perhaps special books for children could be used to help educate teenagers on the subject. "Oh dear, now Cinderella understands why she was supposed to be home by midnight. The Prince still hasn't guessed why she's been throwing up in the mornings." You could have "Willy Wonka and the Family Planning Clinic," "Harry Potter and the Child Support Agency," and "Teletubbies say Uh-oh!" Or how about the pop-up *Joy of Sex*? Obviously after a few years it won't pop up like it used to, but hey, that's life.

More education has to be the answer and hats off to the government for taking a brave stand on this. Obviously it's going to be a struggle to get fourteen-year-old boys to think about sex, but it has to be done. "Oh but Miss, do we have to do sex again, can't we do logarithms, please Miss, please?" It turned out that half of the kids didn't turn up to their very first sex education lesson, but at least they had a decent excuse. They were down at the hospital giving birth to twins.

OFF WITH HER HEAD!

6 July 2002

The British government has finally lost touch. They have finally gone native. Somebody knocks the head off the statue of Lady Thatcher and they somehow try to suggest that this is a bad thing! I completely agree with them that Paul Kellehar should not have removed the head of Thatcher's statue. He should have decapitated the original. It all could have been handled so differently. Tony Blair should have come out into Downing Street looking excited and proud: "I would like to pass you over to our minister for culture, as she has some news I think you might like to hear." The minister would then have stepped forward trying not to look too smug as she read from the prepared statement: "Be pleased to inform her majesty, that at approximately 1200 hours GMT, a lone anticapitalist protester entered the Guildhall in London and knocked Mrs. Thatcher's block off! God save the Queen!"

And above the cheers of the waiting crowds the excited journalists would have fired dozens of questions only to be chastised by the prime minister. "Just rejoice at that news! And congratulate Paul Kellehar and Guildhall's security!"

Instead, the condemnation was universal. "Politics is about persuading people through reason," said Lady Thatcher to the sound of a million jaws dropping around the country. Of course whacking heads with cricket bats is not something that should be encouraged even if it was a technique that Thatcher herself used to persuade more stubborn members of her cabinet from time to time. Foreign commentators have asked why the assailant was not stopped by security when he entered the building carrying a cricket bat. They have to understand that in England, if someone's in possession of a cricket bat it's just presumed that they'll never be able to hit their target. Perhaps this new feature should be incorporated into the English national game; it would certainly liven up the cricket coverage a bit: "And the England captain steps out, swings his bat high, misses the ball completely, but it doesn't matter because he has knocked the head off the Thatcher statue! Marvellous, just listen to that applause! But oh dear, the wicket keeper has managed to catch the head, and he's out!"

Having failed to remove the head with a cricket bat, the protestor used one of the metal poles used to support the fancy bit of crimson rope that is supposed to prevent people from getting too close to the statue. You have to ask questions about the security system in operation here. Those dark red bits of rope have never been much of a deterrent to a really determined trespasser. In 1940 when Hitler was looking for the weak spot in France's famous Maginot Line, he identified the section near the Ardennes that consisted of just a few poles linked together with twirly red rope as offering the least resistance to the Wehrmacht's tank divisions. If I'd been the security guard on duty at the Guildhall, I would have just stuck the head back on with a bit of araldite and hoped nobody would notice.

"Hang on a minute! What's that crack all around the neck with gluey stuff dripping out of it?"

"Honestly! It's supposed to be like that, you philistine. That is the artist's message, about the nature of, er—nothingness."

"Oh right, yeah."

It has to be said that as a work of art the original statue was a pretty vapid effort; if it had been eight inches high it would have been the sort of bland statuette that middle-class ladies place in backlit corner units, on the little shelf above the crystal gondola. Exactly the sort of bland art that Mrs. Thatcher herself might have gone for, in fact. But now with the head removed and lying at her feet, it suddenly feels like a deeply symbolic and ironic statement. The leader who divided British society now lies in two pieces herself. For a woman who lost her marbles years ago, it all seems wonderfully appropriate.

The artist is said to be deeply saddened by what has happened. So would you be if you had to meet up with her all over again for another half dozen sittings. But if a replacement is to be commissioned, shouldn't it be more in keeping with the more radical end of the Brit Art scene? How about Lady Thatcher's unmade bed—with empty whisky bottles and chain-mail knickers strewn across the sheets? Or how about a glass tank containing one of Mrs. Thatcher's lungs pickled in formaldehyde? All right, so it might cause onlookers to recoil with disgust and nausea. But not as much as having an eight-foot-high realistic likeness staring down at you.

TALKING RUBBISH

13 July 2002

This week the government took decisive action to help Britain's sketch writers and cartoonists. They published a great big document on the subject of rubbish. The humorists scratched their heads into the small hours; "Hmmm, there's pages and pages of this thing, all about rubbish; there must be an angle in here somewhere?"

"Nope, beats me."

The headline grabbing idea was that households producing too much waste will have to start paying. It's a brilliant plan; at the moment we're saying, "Please don't drop litter, please take your rubbish home with you." And now we're simply adding, "Oh and it'll cost you £1 a bag every time you do so." What greater incentive could there be to stop people dumping? We've seen what happens when people have to pay to get rid of their old cars or fridges; and all because those lazy dustmen somehow try to claim that they can't put a Nissan Sunny into the back of their cart. Even the Royal Navy has started simply dumping its battleships.* (There's now a great big sticker on H.M.S. *Nottingham* saying "Police Aware.")

Just as skiers go "off-piste" and owners of four-wheel drives go "off-road," this week the captain of the British destroyer H.M.S. Nottingham went "off-sea."

Fortunately in Britain all the appropriate spaces for dumping are very clearly marked; they have a big sign saying "No Dumping." There's something about certain stretches of brick wall that compels people to think, "You know what that spot really needs? A wet mattress and a broken kitchen unit, yup, that would really finish it off." "Super idea—and maybe some tins of hardened paint arranged around the edges?"

Something has to be done about all the rubbish produced in the UK, other than putting it out on cable. Britain has one of the worst waste problems in Europe; we've all seen the ugly pictures of hundreds of tons of rubbish spread everywhere, bin liners split open as mangy-looking seagulls pick over the stinking contents. Yes, that's what happens to the front garden when the dustmen don't get a Christmas tip. If the refuse does eventually get collected it ends up in one of Britain's 1,400 landfill sites (except for all the empty Coke cans, which go in my front yard). Britain has more landfill sites than most countries because of the number of mysterious holes in the ground located close to something once apparently known as "the British Coal industry." So that's why Thatcher closed all the mines; she needed somewhere to put all her husband's empties. It was a brilliant political scam: "All right, coal miners, you can reopen all the coal mines if you want, but you'll have to get all the old disposable nappies out first."

To cut down on the amount of rubbish that we bury, we're going to have to recycle more. It's suggested that people should recycle their vegetable waste by having a compost heap. Fine for some households, but if you're a single parent on the thirteenth floor of a high-rise block you're unlikely to be worrying about whether the avocado skins would make good compost for the begonias. Paper is another obvious area where recycling should be encouraged. In Britain we throw away millions of tons of waste paper every day, and that's just the takeaway Chinese menus. Where I live in South London there is a scheme that involves putting all your newspapers outside your front gate for recycling. Countless hours are wasted every Monday night as couples anxiously argue over which publication would look best on top of the crate before it's put out for all to see:

"You can't just leave *Chat!* magazine on top, what will the neighbours think?"

"But I only put it there to cover up that Outsize Underwear catalogue we got through the post."

"*What Computer?*"

"Too nerdy."

"*The Weekly World News?*"

"God forbid!"

"Look, hang on, the newsagent's still open, I'll pop down and get a copy of the *New York Review of Books*—we can stick that on top."

And then an hour later an old man in a grubby mac walks past and casually throws a copy of *Penthouse* on top of the pile and all the whole street has you marked down as a pervert forevermore. As well as publicly displaying your choice of reading material, you are also forced to advertise your weekly alcohol consumption when you put out the empty wine bottles. All I'm saying is that the Catholic priest on our road must do an awful lot of Holy Communions at home.

In the future anything that is not recycled will be weighed by the dustmen and a levy will be charged on particularly heavy garbage cans. This will have people sneaking bags of rubbish into each other's bins under cover of darkness; at three in the morning the bedroom window will go up, followed by shouts of "Oi neighbour, that's *our* bloody wheelie bin you're loading up there!"

"Oh sorry, Mrs. Blair, it's so hard to see in the dark. Anyway it's not my fault, I've got tons and tons of useless scrap paper to get rid of. It's that huge report on rubbish from your husband."

See, even jokes can be recycled.

COMPUTERISED GIs

20 July 2002

The army is going all high-tech. Now when you phone them up you get a disjointed digital recording saying, "Thank you for phoning the Ministry of Defence. If you wish to declare war on the United Kingdom, please press 1. If you are the American president and require British forces to join your own to give the spurious impression of international cooperation, please press 2. If you wish to register a complaint about the massacre of innocent civilians, press 3 or hold for an operator." In which case you have to listen to Vivaldi for thirty years until someone's finally prepared to listen.

This week it was announced that British service personnel are to be armed with all the latest microchip technology to assist them in the war against terrorism. With so much of today's defence budget being spent on computerised military hardware, they needed that extra £3.5 billion to pay for the printer cartridges. Modelling the "soldier of the future" outfit for the BBC News was an embarrassed-looking soldier weighed down by countless electrical gadgets strapped all over his body, while his face seemed to say, "I haven't the faintest bloody idea how any of this stuff works." There were satellite communicators, computerised weapons, an integrated monitor screen just above his eye line, all in standard army camouflage colours making the soldier impossible to pick out until the moment his mobile phone suddenly went off, playing the *Great Escape* theme at full volume.

Of course with the soldiers now carrying the latest in communications technology, terrorists will not be their only enemy. They're also going to have to watch their backs for teenage boys mugging them for their million-pound digital equipment that they could flog down at the pub for a tenner. The computer packs are specially designed to be light and highly mobile; it's just a shame that carrying all those enormous manuals are going to slow them down so much.

Yet the whole point of all this increased communications software is supposed to be speed. Soon NATO forces will be able to blow up the wrong building far more quickly than they have been able to do in the past. The ground forces will be in constant communication with reconnaissance aircraft, unmanned aerial vehicles, and attack helicopters, right up until the moment the computer crashes and then all the aircraft crash as well.

But of course the test of all this technology will be the first time that this soldier is on the battlefield face-to-face with an enemy gun-man. A split second can make the difference between life or death as he activates his computerised weaponry. But it doesn't take out the enemy; instead a little reminder wizard appears on-screen: "Click here to register your Microsoft Anti-Terrorist software for great technical support, free upgrades, and special offers on other Microsoft products." The soldier frantically clicks the 'register later' icon as enemy bullets fly past his head. Grenades are now exploding on either side of him, as a smiling little animated Mr. Bomb character bounces up and down on the screen saying, "Are you sure you want to register later?"

That's if the technology works at all, of course. It's one thing to have your printer refusing to respond when you were hoping to catch the last post. But I'd say you'd get even more annoyed with modern technology when you are being surrounded by Taliban gunmen and the computerised missile launcher says "Error in weapon configuration—refer to helpline." It's at times like this that you wish you'd sent that guarantee card back to Hewlett Packard.

With our armed forces increasingly dependent on computer software it won't be germ warfare we are worried about, but virus warfare. "Oh look, I've got an e-mail from someone called Osama—I'll just open that attachment and see what it is!" says the soldier brightly as the entire NATO communications network goes down. Or maybe the enemy will be closer to home. I can't help worrying that the boys who left school to become soldiers tended not to be the same boys who were really brilliant with computers. The nervous brainy kids were forced to avoid all the tough boys by going to the computer club every lunchtime, and will have spent the last fifteen years working their way up through the software industry patiently planning their revenge. So when the tattooed meathead of a soldier is stuck in an Iraqi battlefield and has to rely on his computer equipment to save his life he'll suddenly find his software freezing as a voice from the past pops up on the monitor: "Hello Slugger; Timothy Johnson here, from Form 4B. You probably won't remember that every day for five years you broke my glasses and threw my violin case on top of the bus shelter. Well, now you are really going to wish you hadn't. Click here to leave a farewell message on Enemies Reunited."

NEVER MIND THE TERRORISTS, IT'S THE ACCOUNTANTS I'M WORRIED ABOUT

27 July 2002

There was a major scandal on Wall Street this week when a rogue U.S. corporation was found *not* to have been fiddling with its books. "We can't imagine how this has been allowed to happen," said the shamefaced auditors. The chief financial officer immediately resigned in disgrace as it was revealed that the firm's profits were exactly what he'd claimed they were, with no trace of false accounting or the artificial inflation of share prices. However it's thought the chances of this happening in other U.S. corporations remains very slim.

The only thing that is surprising about the wave of financial scandals engulfing America is that everyone is so surprised. Well who'd have thought it—the most aggressive capitalists making inexplicably huge profits turn out to have been cheating! You stop regulating big business and the directors take advantage to make themselves huge illicit fortunes! And we'd all thought they'd made those extra billions by doing a paper route every morning before work.

The most common method of fraud has been to artificially inflate share prices by exaggerating company profits. Suspicions should have been raised when the revenue for the last financial year was given by an eight-year-old boy who excitedly announced the official figure to be a billion, trillion, gillion, quillion, zillion! Or when the figure at the end of the annual report had two zeros scrawled on the end in red felt-tip pen.

For a country obsessed by crime, the Americans are having to learn that criminals come in a variety of guises. Police officers are now making up for lost time as public opinion turns against the new hate figures in U.S. society. America's isolated accountant community, for many years shunned due to their strange stripy suits and incomprehensible language, is now being openly persecuted. "We're not all fraudsters. . . ." implored a spokesman for the accountants. "In fact only 3.34 percent of us in the last fiscal quarter, rising in line with projected forecasts . . ." he went on, but already he seemed to be losing the journalists' attention. Secret video footage has just been released showing traffic cops dragging an innocent auditor out of his car and beating him up. "Thought you could offset projected profit shortfall by excluding capital outlay, huh, you four-eyed geek?" [punch!] "Trying to overstate company revenues by hiding loan repayments eh? God, you pinstripe punks make me sick. . . ." [kick!]

In the nearby financial district, auditors reacted angrily, not rioting exactly, but the nearest equivalent for accountants. Desks were left untidy, computer keyboards were left uncovered by polythene dust sheets, calculators were left switched on, lids left off fountain pens. . . . Witnesses said they had not seen such untidy scenes since the great double-entry ledger protests of '68.

Now the ratings of *America's Most Wanted* look set to plummet. The only reconstruction so far showed a man sitting at his desk for a long time in front of a computer. "Does this jog any memories?" said the presenter as millions of viewers rang in to say they had a vague memory of witnessing a similar scene.

As the stock markets crashed, millions of ordinary citizens lost their pensions and savings and George Bush announced that he would take tough action to deal with whoever had done so much damage to American interests. U.S. bombers were dispatched to mete out the usual punishment, but then were swiftly called back when it was explained to the president that the perpetrators worked on Wall Street and bombing New York might not go down too well right now.

So then his advisors sat him down and very slowly explained the nature of modern corporate fraud from start to finish, finally declaring, "So you see, Mr. President, that's why billions of dollars have now disappeared."

"I understand. So did anyone see the getaway car?"

"No it wasn't stolen, sir. It was fraud."

"So these are counterfeit dollars we're looking for. Do we have the numbers?"

"Sir, it's not real money, these are just figures in a computer."

"Geez they shouldn't have left the money in the computer, that's always the first thing these guys steal."

The reason that this crisis is so damaging to the president is that this sort of unfettered capitalism is exactly what the Global Village Idiot is all about. Not only is he the champion of unregulated business, but Enron and its like also paid for his election campaign. Maybe it was Enron's auditors who counted up the ballot papers that handed him victory after getting fewer votes than his opponent. Bush has promised to be tough on these superrich fraudsters so we can expect them to go to prison for the rest of their days. But something tells me that America's billionaires will receive less punishment than an ordinary U.S. citizen would. Of course wiping out the pensions and savings for millions of ordinary people is a crime that deserves the sack. But once they're unemployed let's just hope they don't make any false claims for minor Social Security payments because then they'd really be in trouble.

RATS!

3 August 2002

Yesterday cinemas around the country began showing a new horror film. In its final terrifying scene a pretty girl awakens in bed to find herself covered in a plague of filthy rats. Yes, it's the latest new release from those well-known purveyors of extreme horror action—the Keep Britain Tidy Campaign.

No one can accuse them of being at all sensationalist about this. All they are saying in this new advert is that if you drop litter you'll wake up with rats crawling all over your face—it's a very reasonable and moderate statement. "We don't want to alarm you, but you drop one apple core and huge mutant rodents with razor-sharp teeth will swarm out of the sewers to gnaw through your skull and suck out your brains while you sleep." And the cinema goers all shrug and spill another kilo of popcorn all over the floor.

Apparently the making of this commercial was a rather tense affair for the casting agency concerned. "So what's the part?" said the rats as they turned up for rehearsals. "Are we the adorably furry pets that comfort the kiddies in the children's hospital? Or is it a Stuart Little type thing, cute rat with voiceover from Billy Crystal?"

"Er, no, no . . . it's pretty straightforward, we just wanted you look-ing a bit dirty, nibbling a discarded hot dog."

An awkward hush fell over the thespian rats.

"So we're playing vermin again, are we?" they said tersely.

"Well that is sort of what the advert's about."

"I see. It's just as members of the rat community we do get a bit fed up with being typecast, I mean we rats do other things apart from breed in the sewers and scamper round spreading diseases, you know."

And the rats stormed off to their trailers to ring their agents but then were distracted by some rotting burgers on the way.

This advert is required because so many people are discarding fast food cartons that the rats are coming out of the sewers to feed on leftover McDonald's. So if the poison doesn't kill them then there's always heart disease. Apparently rats love the meat from fast food outlets; now it seems they're cannibals as well. Now rats are back as public enemy number one. Britain can no longer be a soft touch for rats; politicians are suggesting that rats be confined to secure deten-tion centers while their claims to be genuine rodents are processed. Others say our hostility is based on myth and ignorance. There are now officially 60 million rats in the UK, and that's just the ones that bothered to return their census forms. Every year 200 of this number pass on Weil's disease to humans; so as always, it's just a small mi-nority who give all the others a bad name. In fact British rats would have done well to fire their PR company years ago. When fleas gave everyone the bubonic plague, their spin doctor put out a story saying it was all the rats' fault and the brand "rat" never really recovered. In any case the creatures involved were the black rat (*Rattus rattus*—it was late on Friday afternoon at the rodent naming office), which was later displaced by the brown rat (*Rattus norvegicus*—named after the first Stranglers album). But still all these years later it is presumed that the only good rat is a dead rat. Britain's domestic cat community has been censured for failing to do their bit to keep down the vermin population. At a press conference this week a spokesman for the cats seemed unmoved by the criticism. "Yeah, what of it?" he shrugged before going back to sleep again.

Meanwhile increasingly cruel means are being employed to poison, trap, and eradicate rats and nobody cares. Where are the fifty-something women who never had kids, weeping outside the ministry? Where are the balaclava-clad hard men of the Animal Liberation Front ready to burn down the rat poison factory? The British public has studied this issue very carefully and has concluded that any way you look at it, rats are just not as cute as dolphins and baby seals. Cruelty against fluffy doe-eyed animals is one thing—but smelly disgusting rats, well sorry, you had it coming to you, I'm afraid.

But with fox hunting successfully banned the solution to Britain's rat problem seems obvious. Could there be a more pleasing sight in the English countryside than dozens of huntsmen resplendent in their bright red tunics, disappearing into the sewers and getting covered in crap? What could do more to gladden the hearts of an Englishman than seeing the master of the hunt clambering out of a manhole, wiping the brown sludge from his jodhpurs? Soon we can look forward to our towns echoing with the sound of the huntsman's horn telling us that a traditional rat hunt has begun in earnest. It will be a signal announcing that the rural upper classes have just clambered into our sewers: a noise that says, "Right—everyone flush now!"

SOCCER FANS
ARE REVOLTING

10 August 2002

Today is the first day of the English football season. Up and down the country will be heard that traditional cry of nonfans saying, "Already? But it had only just finished!" In recent years the popularity of the sport has mushroomed beyond all expectations; violence is down, racist chanting is rare, and the quality of the matches is significantly better. But still some commentators go all misty-eyed about times gone by: "Oh, it's not the same these days, I mean, when I was a lad, you'd be packed into the terraces behind a seven-foot chain smoker, unable to see your team draw nil-nil after the defenders kept passing back to the keeper and then on the way home you'd get beaten up for wearing the wrong scarf by that bloke who'd been shouting racist abuse. Ah, happy days . . ."

But a decade on from the formation of the Premier League, the majority of clubs that were left behind are now in trouble. The collapse of ITV digital and the subsequent resignations have left the football league in crisis. Supporters watching games this afternoon may already notice the lower division clubs making one or two economies. Unable to afford proper kits, players will be wearing embarrassingly tight shirts and huge baggy shorts from the lost property basket.

The ball will be a plastic one from Woolworth's with Harry Potter on the side and when it's kicked out of the ground, the rush goalie will be forced to go round and ask that grumpy old man next door, "Excuse me, can we have our ball back, please?" Final score two-nil. "It wasn't two-nil, that second one was a post—it went straight over my jumper." "No, it would have gone in-off!"

Another worry for the Football League is that while arrests are down in the Premier League, according to tables published yesterday they actually increased in the lower divisions. No wonder there's no demand for coverage of the minor soccer games; the broadcasters boasted that their interactive coverage made it just like being at a real match. So when you leapt off the sofa to celebrate your team's goal they supplied a couple of opposing fans to beat you up. You have to question the wisdom of publishing league tables for football arrests. Did they imagine the perpetrators would weep with remorse at being brandished the worst troublemakers in the land? "I'm so dashed upset, Tarquin, we've really let down the vast majority of genuine peaceloving sports fans at our club." "Yes Julian, the shame of it! I'll never be able to show my face down at my men's anger management workshop again."

Or is there perhaps an outside chance that the Neanderthals might take some sort of perverse pride in being top of the arrests league? Maybe the police could arrange a pitched battle between the fans who finished third and fourth to decide who gets a playoff place. In fact football violence roughly fits the Marxist analysis of war between capitalist economies. While working-class fans are beating each other up, the real enemy, football's ruling class, remains safe in their corporate boxes and chairmen's suites becoming multimillionaires as they bring poverty to the poorer clubs. Well this season it's all going to change. Suddenly aware of their own strength the supporters of the world will unite and throw off the chains of having to pay £45 for a replica shirt that cost 10p to produce in some sweatshop in China. Instead of pointlessly attacking each other, the newly politicised fans will storm the Manchester United Directors Box, declaring the people's first socialist soccer soviet. The superrich chairmen of the big clubs will be lined up and shot, but they'll survive because English centre forwards are doing the shooting.

A supporter's revolution would slightly change the game, of course. "Quick pass!" "Sorry comrade, but such a move would have to be ratified by the people's executive committee!" But by bringing Marxist doctrine to the Premier League we'll prove that socialism is the only way forward for the rest of our society. "The workers! United! Will never be defeated—because frankly a score draw is always the fairest result!" And imagine the thrilling climax to the season when you know every club will finish with the exact same number of points and identical goal difference. Er, hang on, I think I'd better think this out again. . . .

I'M A WORLD LEADER,
GET ME OUT OF HERE!

30 August 2002

All week a conference centre in Johannesburg has been host to many of the most important people in the world. The security has been incredibly tight. One man who was thrown out is still hanging around outside the compound insisting that he is a bona fide delegate. "I'm not making it up! There really is such a country as Turkmenistan!" Meanwhile the girl at the reception desk has been having a terrible time trying to deal with all the complaints from the Western leaders who jumped at this chance to fly away in August. "What do you mean it's winter in the Southern Hemisphere? It's just not good enough. . . ."

In reality this convention is not much different than any conference of middle managers taking place at the Holiday Inn in Newark, New Jersey. The reps all file in, collect their little name badges, and then excitedly check their hotel rooms.

"Ooh, a trouser press!" says a thrilled Gerhard Schroeder. "And look, miniature packets of cashew nuts in the minibar!" exclaims the Russian delegate, as he pops the free shower cap and little sewing kit into his suitcase. During the first session all the world leaders sit there with anxious faces. Not because they are worrying about global ecology, but because they're all privately thinking, "If I watch the adult channel in my room tonight, will it come up on my bill as 'Pay Movie' or 'Pervy Porn Flick'?"

The first talk is done by a Scandinavian environment minister using Microsoft Powerpoint: "So you see that within fifty years, Earth will be unable to sustain life and we will all be dead." On the screen a little animated graphic shows the world expand and then go *Pop!* and everyone gasps and turns to the delegate beside them.

"Ooh that's clever, isn't it!"

"Yes, I can't do anything like that on my computer. . . ."

After the coffee break there's a talk on teamwork and motivation from a retired sports star and then in the afternoon they've arranged for some workshops.

"Right, if you chaps from the Balkans could get into small groups. . . ."

"We already are."

"And if the South Americans can choose a team leader, no, don't use the army to install him."

Soon they are all ready for the trust exercises. "The Israeli minister here is going to fall backwards and these Arab leaders are going to catch him. You look a bit worried, Binyamin. . . ."

By the end of the day they can't wait to get out of there and sit down to the evening meal, especially with the promise of a professional comedian as an after-dinner speaker. For some reason the stand-up comic seems to struggle as he pauses during each joke for the various interpreters attempting to translate all the set-ups. The whole dinner might have been more tactfully arranged. The Western leaders had a huge slap-up five-course feast while over on the third world table the waiters just dumped a sack of dried milk powder and left them to fight over it.

Back at home the ordinary voters remain cynical about their leaders' ability to change anything. People need to see their representatives getting stuck in and really making the best of a difficult situation, so next time the gathering will take a completely different format. Coming soon on the BBC is a brand-new docu-soap: *I'm a World Leader, Get Me Out of Here!* In order to understand the problems of the environment more fully, presidents and prime ministers will be forced to live in poverty in a hostile tropical setting, while the hosts laugh at their efforts and dish out the next challenge. "Oh no! The Canadian president has got dysentery from drinking that polluted water! And now he's got to go to the toilet in front of everyone!" they will chuckle. "Whoops! Jacques Chirac has been bitten by a mosquito and now he's got malaria! I bet now he was wishing he hadn't cut back French medical aid to Africa!" they'll giggle.

Of course George Bush won't turn up again. Just like the original TV show, only D-list celebs will be available, and viewers will be left saying, "Who on earth is that?" as the prime minister of Bhutan flirts with the president of Luxembourg. But that is the trouble with the whole Johannesburg conference—the people who really count aren't even there. Not just George Bush, whose country alone is responsible for the largest proportion of the world's greenhouse gases, but all the unaccountable people who run the global corporations and multinationals that are now more powerful and damaging than many nation-states. So perhaps the only really effective way to help the environment and developing countries would be to get all the corporate billionaires to Johannesburg. If they saw the security they would be reassured of their own safety. "That should keep people out . . ." they'd say, looking at all the razor wire, the lines of electrified fences, and the heavily policed concrete barriers.

"What are you talking about?" would come the reply. "That's to keep you in here."

FRENCH LESSONS

2 November 2002

J acques Chirac lost his temper with Tony Blair this week, call-ing the prime minister "rude"' and cancelling the scheduled Anglo-French summit. All Tony had said was, "So how did France get on in the World Cup?"* For a French president to call a British leader "rude" is a bit like England accusing the French of having warm beer. One of the problems was that Tony Blair insisted that he'd got a B in his AP French and said he was per-fectly capable of conducting the summit without a translator. So the prime minister asked the French president straight out, "Brother Jacques, Brother Jacques, are you sleeping?" Things went from bad to worse when he added, "Voulez-vous couchez avec moi, ce soir?"

The French have still not forgiven Britain for the diplomatic di-sasters of last year. It began with Britain's deputy prime minister being a bit patronising toward his French counterpart. As the UN talks on climate change fell apart, she screamed, "Unless we act now most of

---

*The reigning world champions crashed out of the 2002 World Cup without even scoring a single goal. When I commiserated with the owner of my local French café, Monsieur le Patron explained that it was because a lot of the French team played in England. Of course! It was our fault!

the world's land mass will be underwater, oxygen will disappear, and the entire planet will suffocate!" And the British minister said "All right love, all right. It's not the end of the world. . . ."

Tony Blair tried to smooth things over by taking Jacques Chirac out for lunch to a pub in his constituency but things hit rock bottom when the French president was greeted with the words, "Hello, welcome to a traditional English restaurant. Today's special comes with a medley of diced vegetables and Yorkshire pudding." It was of course a calculated piece of revenge by the British government. They could have retaliated against the French outburst by cancelling trade talks or banning French imports, but no, far more vicious to buy Chirac a glass of wine from a British pub. And then film him drinking it. "Any more attacks on my deputy," said Tony, "and we'll be using the British public transport system to get back to the airport."

This new dispute erupted over plans to reform the Common Agricultural Policy. The tabloid editorial teams wrestled for hours about the angle to take on this story. Which way should they go: explaining the complex subsidies of the Common Agriculture Policy that have underwritten European food producers and undercut third world farmers? Or just say that Chirac is a typical garlic-smelling frog with terrible personal hygiene who'd beg the plucky Brits to bail them out again as soon as there was another world war?

Anglo-French relations have been precarious ever since 1066 when King Harold asked the Normans what they were doing in Sussex and they stuck an arrow in his eye, which is only marginally less cooperative than most of the French guards on the London-to-Paris Eurostar today. The Normans then went backpacking round their newly conquered land, and if you look closely at the Bayeux tapestry you can make out lots of little figures spitting out warm beer and laughing at the primitive public transport facilities. Then in the fourteenth century thousands of Englishmen were persuaded to join the army fighting the French. "Darling, I'm going off to fight in the Hundred Years' War . . ." "When will you be back?" "I dunno, it could be ages. . . ." (The Hundred Years' War actually lasted 116 years, but the last sixteen years were spent arguing over which language the peace treaty should be in.) Things got worse when Joan of Arc decided to drive out all the posh English people who had holiday cottages in Normandy. She was then burnt to a cinder by the English, to the horror of the French who thought that two minutes on either side would have been plenty. Then Henry V took a couple of thousand English troops (plus an excellent speechwriter) over the channel before winning a famous victory and coming back loaded up with lots of little bottles of French lager and a big piece of Brie for the missus. After that the two countries fought wars with all the regularity of football tournaments, with the difference that the French didn't win quite so often. The last big bust-up ended with the Battle of Waterloo, precipitating a hundred years of unchallenged British supremacy and a number-one hit for ABBA.

Except that is not how history is viewed on the other side of the channel. I recently found myself chatting with a French woman and the subject turned to the French attitude toward the United States. "I think the French feel hostile to the Americans . . ." she said, "because before the rise of the United States, the most powerful country in the world was France."

There was a slight pause while I picked myself up off the floor. "Sorry?" I said. "When was this exactly?"

"Before America was the major world power, it was France."

Obviously as a liberal and an internationalist I don't care who was the major world power before America, it just so happens that it was Great Britain, that's all. She countered my amusing interpretation of history by reminding me of the French Empire in North Africa. "That was all desert!" I exploded. "Now yer British Empire, that was a proper empire, India, Australia, South Africa, Canada, why the sun never set. . . ." I went on as the strains of "God Save the Queen" rose behind me and Union Jack tattoos popped out all over my skin. European liberals have a duty to recognise the shameful inheritance of our imperialist history. But the French had better accept that we've got a bigger imperialist tradition to be ashamed of than they have.

The historical baggage that we British carry around with us is of course the real reason that we struggle to accept the increased status of the French in Europe. What's really underneath all this week's anti-French rhetoric is the nagging resentment that France and Germany are now the dominant partners in Europe; we have clung to an overinflated view of ourselves that has left us as bit part players in the shaping of the European Union.

So in terms of domestic popularity it won't damage Tony Blair to fall out with Jacques Chirac. But this spat does not come at a good time for the European project as a whole. Negotiations are currently under way regarding the expansion of the EU to include countries such as Poland and Hungary, which is widely supported by British cabinet ministers because it would mean their au pairs would no longer be staying here illegally. Meanwhile, one of Chirac's prede- cessors has just published a draft constitution for the EU, carefully worded to stir up the paranoia of the British anti-Europeans. Among his suggestions for the future of Europe are the election of a Euro- pean president. Whatever the merits of this idea, the prospect of lots of endless god-awful cartoons in the papers featuring badly drawn Adolf Hitlers and Napoleons might make it more than we can bear. These proposals represent something of a comeback for Valery Giscard d'Estaing, who failed to retain the French presidency when

it was realised that he had a girl's name. Other controversial suggestions were that the European Union consider adopting a new title
(he thought the name "France" had a certain ring to it).

The British reaction to the falling-out of Blair and Chirac under-
lines a deeper problem with the whole concept of European integra-
tion. There is no such thing as European patriotism. While people
can be proud to be Scottish and British, or proud to be Californian
and American, it's hard to imagine us sneering at the continent of
Antarctica for being not as good as Europe.

A few years back there began an attempt to improve understanding between two of the continent's historical rivals by organising
school exchange visits, in which French teenagers were apparently
supposed to endear themselves to us by wearing cagoules and wandering around London shoplifting. The idea of the cultural exchange
has now been extended into a scheme under which the French send
us their brilliant soccer players and we send them mad cow disease.

Perhaps the way to achieve greater understanding at the highest
level is for our top politicians to do French exchanges as well. Tony
should have to go and stay with Jacques's family for a couple of weeks
and vice versa. Imagine what it would do for Anglo-French relations
to have the PM spending a fortnight in a Parisian suburb taking up
smoking and whizzing round on a little moped without a helmet.
Then for the return visit Chirac could meet all of Tony's friends: "This
is Jacques, everyone . . ." Tony will say and all the girls in the cabinet will gasp and swoon as the cool French boy raises an eyebrow and
casually lights up a Gitanes. Obviously there might be the risk of a
diplomatic incident when on the last day of his trip Jacques is ar-
rested for shoplifting in Carnaby Street. Stuffed into the pockets of
his cagoule, the police will discover one stolen London shaky-snow
scene, a Beatles key ring, and an ashtray from the Hard Rock Café.
But by now Blair and Chirac will be lifelong friends. And what's more,

Tony can say, "Right, Jacques, either you agree to reform the European Union, or we're telling your parents."

Perhaps as part of the final stage of Euro-integration, French and British cultures should become fully entwined. Britain will have to listen to French pop music, and the French will have to keep their underpants on in the sauna. The French will have to watch *Animal Hospital* on the BBC but the English will have to let them eat any of the animals that don't make it. But Europe has no choice but to learn to get along. Racism can have no place in the future of the continent; and so let France and Britain lead the way in doing away with chauvinism and petty nationalism. And then the British press will proudly boast of how we built a Europe free of intolerance, xenophobia, and bigotry, how everyone learned to love one another irrespective of race or creed. "If racial prejudice is what you're into . . ." the tabloids will say, "Frankly, you'd be far better off with those bloody krauts."

GIVE THANKS THAT BRITAIN DOESN'T HAVE THANKSGIVING

28 November 2002

Today is Thanksgiving Day in the United States. The Pilgrim Fathers were so grateful that their first harvest had been safely gathered they decided to have a special holiday in which everyone could give thanks to God by getting into their cars and sitting in a traffic jam. Given current trends it is quite likely that Thanksgiving Day will be imposed upon Britain as another Hallmark holiday within the next twenty years. It falls conveniently midway between Halloween and Christmas and would fill a yawning gap in the shops' promotional timetable that currently has Christmas stretching right back to early autumn. American consumerism has always been one step ahead. Instead of spending eight weeks gearing their customers up for buying one turkey, they slot in an extra festival at the end of November so everyone has to buy another one four weeks beforehand. It cannot be long before British shops try this scam on us.

Ten years ago Halloween was not a commercial event in the United Kingdom until "trick or treating" was imported from the United States. Now we are subjected to the horrific sight of plastic goblin masks at the terrifying price of £2.50 each and are forced to buy variety packs of fun-size chocolate bars (£3.99) to give to calling children if we do not want our front doors sprayed with spooky spider-web spray (small cans, £1.99 each). If there is a week in the calendar where there is nothing obvious to flog us, the shops will make something up. Father's Day was invented by an American greeting card company and there was actually a genuine attempt by the same people to launch a "Secretary's Day," when employers could express their thanks to their overworked assistants. This one never really took off, presumably because the bosses kept sending their secretaries out to buy the cards they were going to give them. Giving presents on birthdays is a development of this century. It seems that the cynical capitalists will never miss an opportunity to flog you with something—a point that I made in my first novel, *The Best a Man Can Get,* an excellent Christmas gift at only £6.99.

Since most of the significant days in our calendar were originally Christian festivals it is no wonder that these are the dates that the new religion of consumerism has seized for itself. The resurrection of Christ is celebrated by buying lots and lots of overpackaged chocolate eggs, obviously. The martyrdom of St. Valentine is remembered by the doubling of flower prices. The church has no right to complain about the way their holy days have been hijacked by the new religion of shopping, because latching onto the festivals of existing religions was exactly how Christianity got itself established. "Yuletide is just becoming too Christian these days," said the pagans, bemoaning the way the winter sacrifice at Stonehenge was being spoilt by a class of five-year-olds singing "Silent Night." Many of the ways that we once celebrated the birth of Christ predate his arrival. In pre-Roman Britain it was traditional during the winter festival that elderly relatives would come and stay for far too long, turn up the heating, and nick all the macadamias from the bowl of nuts on the sideboard. We no longer acknowledge the shortest day of the year, perhaps because now it feels like the longest when you are watching *It's a Wonderful Life* for the twentieth bloody time.

So just as the winter solstice gave way to a celebration of the birth of Christ, the new religion of shopping has made the whole of December its holy month. The modern cathedrals of the Miracle Mile are packed with worshipers. "Lo! I bring news of great joy to all mankind. Wal-Mart is doing Pokémon Blue Nintendos at £24.99." The spending frenzy builds to a fervent climax by Christmas Eve as panic sets in because for one day of the year the shops are going to close. But fear not, sales start 9 A.M. December 26—and then millions of people go shopping all over again. The real shopping fundamentalists get into their sleeping bags and camp outside the department stores so they can be first to hear the joyful ringing of the tills. They sleep on the streets alongside all the people who have been bankrupted by the whole crazy money-go-round.

And that is the problem with the rampant consumerism that has become the hollow substitute for any spiritual depth in our lives. Just like the church before it, consumerism promises a happiness that it cannot deliver. Heaven was in the next life, not this one. The eternal fulfillment promised by the ownership of a Sega Dreamcast is out of reach for most people. But still we are presented with more and more things that we feel we must buy and more shopping festivals in our calendar on which we should buy them.

Today in the holy land of consumerism, everyone will overindulge on roast turkey and pumpkin pie. We should just be grateful that for the time being we are spared that one particular burden on our overstretched family budgets. So let's give thanks that we don't have Thanksgiving. Great idea, say the shops, we could have a special day when we do this. How about the last Thursday in November—shops are open until midnight.

WEAPONS OF
MASS DISTRACTION

30 November 2002

After four long years the United Nations weapons inspectors this week resumed their search for those hidden Iraqi weapons of mass destruction. With their hands still over their eyes they breathlessly counted: ". . . nine million, nine hundred and ninety-nine thousand, nine hundred and ninety nine . . . TEN MILLION! Com-ing!" How Saddam giggled as he watched them peeking in the cupboard under the stairs and behind the curtains. "Cold . . . cold . . . ooh, getting warmer; no, cold again. Freezing!" But after a while it got a bit embarrassing for the Iraqi president having them snoop all over the place. "What's in this drawer?" "Ooh no, don't look in there!" And they pulled it open only to find a pair of old underpants with "Sex Machine" emblazoned across the front. "Look, they were a joke birthday present from my brother. I never wear them, honest."

The work of the weapons inspectors is supposed to be top secret, giving the Iraqis absolutely no warning about which sites are to be visited. So there was a mild suspicion that they might possibly have been bugged when the first location they visited displayed a big banner saying "Baghdad Fertilizer Plant Welcomes the UN Weapons Inspectors!" and a choir of local schoolchildren sang a specially composed anthem as the delegates were directed toward the buffet lunch. Would that explain the wires trailing from the large bunch of flowers that was placed in the middle of their conference table? Is that why they were given a free mobile phone with their car rental?

First they had to decide where they were going to look. They tried driving around a bit but despite all the helpful signs marking tourist sites on the motorway, not one said "Nuclear Bomb Factory" next to a little picture of a mushroom cloud. They tried photocopying a picture of a missile and attaching it to a few lampposts with the caption "Lost! Huge Chemical Warhead, Answers to the Name of 'Scud'." Of course when you're looking for something you may never find it but at least you come across a few other things that you thought you'd lost for good. So far the UN team has uncovered three Polly Pocket figures, a marble, the instructions to the tumble dryer, and a plastic clip that they think probably came with the microscooter. "Oh look, a ten-franc coin; is that still legal tender? Um, I don't think so, but put it back in the kitchen drawer just in case." But George Bush needs no further evidence. "Imagine if these items fell into the hands of Iraq's elite Republican Guard!" "You could have someone's eye out with that!" said Colin Powell, examining the sharp plastic edge of the charger from an old mobile phone. The reporting of the inspectors' discoveries leaves us in no doubt of Saddam's guilt. They have found paper cups of a type that would be used to refresh workers making weapons of mass destruction. Also uncovered was an atlas that included detailed maps of the United States and Britain and a keyboard that could be used to type the letters "B-O-M-B." Whatever they find, the verdict is already decided. Even if they unearth no glowing vats of kryptonite it will prove that Saddam has hidden them all away in his cousin's lockup garage. The inspectors are there for appearance's sake, to give the impression of a legitimate process, like an investigation into police brutality or the recounts in Florida.

Since the UN team are completely wasting their time would it not be more worthwhile to get them searching for something a little more useful? "After two weeks hunting in British shopping centers, the United Nations weapons inspectors have finally located some Beyblades at Toys 'R' Us, Merry Hill, Birmingham. Oh no, apparently they've just been sold." Perhaps they could find us an unbreakable CD case or a program on the History Channel that wasn't about the Nazis.

Or maybe they could find that international law that says that one nation has the right to decide there will be a "regime change" in another country thousands of miles away. The whole world would like to see Saddam Hussein overthrown by his own people, but Bush needs this easy battle to help him win the really big fight the following year. Dubya's only interest in foreign policy is what it can do for him at home, now that they're more than halfway through the presidential electoral cycle. So if I were a UN weapons inspector I'd go back to the hotel, empty the minibar, and hope there were enough miniature Johnny Walker bottles to drown the realisation that I was a diplomatic patsy for the U.S. Republican Party. Only I wouldn't stay there too long because there'll definitely be plenty of weapons of mass destruction all over Iraq pretty soon. They'll be dropping from U.S. bombers to mark the start of the American presidential campaign, to make sure there's certainly no "regime change" at the White House. If the inspectors can't see that, then frankly they're never going to spot anything.

MISS WORLD
SHOWS HER AGE

7 December 2002

Tonight in London around a hundred women will parade up and down in their swimming costumes until the judges finally select the most beautiful of them all. No, it's not advertising executives interviewing for their new receptionist, but the Miss World competition returning to Britain in the most controversial of circumstances. The original venue in Nigeria had to be abandoned after the event prompted rioting, arson, and murder. Miss Wales commented, "It is a shame that a small minority of people spoiled it for everyone else. . . ." Well said, that woman! It's always the way, isn't it? Just a small handful of troublemakers who have to go and murder more than two hundred people and leave thousands injured or homeless. The Nigerian government had originally been very keen to stage the contest as they hoped it would show their country in a good light. So that worked well then.

There were no prizes for guessing which nation would step in at the last minute to stage the most embarrassing, anachronistic event in the international calender. Sydney got the Olympics, Germany gets the World Cup, but Britain has Miss World. Obviously the logistics of getting more than a hundred foreign contestants from Africa into Britain at short notice presented quite a few problems. The organisers were assured by that Turkish lorry driver that for just two hundred dollars and a big box of ciggies he could smuggle them all through the channel tunnel, no questions asked. But when it came to it he just turfed them out of the back of the truck at the French coast and told them to cling on to the London train as it sped into the tunnel. It's at times like this that one realizes that national costumes were not designed with practicality in mind.

Eventually the girls were rounded up by immigration officials in England who asked them a series of tough questions, every one of which was met with the answer, "I'd like to travel and work with children. . . ."

"Come on, tell us the truth, what are you hoping for?" snarled the officer.

"World peace," beamed Miss Uruguay, glancing left and right and looking slightly puzzled that there was no applause.

Finally they were allowed to proceed to London, and as a hundred beauty queens boarded the train for Victoria, dozens of middle-aged businessmen were seen optimistically moving their briefcases from the empty train seat beside them. Some feared that the British girls might exploit their home advantage but in fact they could not have gone further out of their way to assist their rivals. They helpfully advised contestants visiting our shores for the first time that the best way to get a really good agent is to stick your photo in telephone boxes with your mobile number clearly marked. Miss Croatia was given lodgings with a Hampstead family, but she's not being allowed to the contest this evening because she's got a huge pile of ironing to finish after she's picked up the kids from ballet.

This competition is now fifty-two years old and frankly the lines started to show some time ago. Despite the Botox and facelifts, there's no denying that poor Miss World has seen better days. This year the

PR could not have been worse if Miss USA had insisted that Miss Iraq could take part only with a bucket over her head. But despite all the controversy the promoters have been doing their best to try to whip up some excitement. One bookies advert proclaimed, "Place a bet and win a pwooarr-tune!" Ouch, my ribs are still aching from this joke. (Miss England is second favourite to win at 20–1, and you can get an each-way bet on the winner marrying a soccer star.) There have been some people who have suggested that with so many deaths in Nigeria the event should be abandoned altogether, but these are probably the very same killjoys who for some reason wanted to cancel the Soweto Al Johnson Tribute Show. One commentator said, "The girls will be wearing swimwear dripping with blood." That's the last time they get Damien Hurst to design the outfits.

In fact a few of the more sensitive contestants withdrew some time ago. Some have returned now that there's been a change in venue, which is a disappointing setback in the battle against sexism and patronising attitudes toward women—but then you know what they say about a woman's prerogative to change her mind. The original boycott was to protest against the sentence passed on Amina Lowal, a Nigerian woman condemned to be stoned to death for having sex outside marriage. And now that hundreds have died in Nigeria as a result of this competition, there is something distasteful about the remaining contestants claiming that what they want most is "world peace." There's only one way for the organisers to salvage any dignity out of this farce—tonight in her absence they should crown Amina Lowal and see if the Nigerians would dare execute a reigning Miss World. But tell the soccer stars not to propose to this one. . . .

ELECTION BATTLE

28 December 2002

I n the United States it is the custom to include in your Christmas card an annual update on all the things that your family has been up to during the previous twelve months. Needless to say, this practice has become the excuse for highly selective reporting, thinly veiled boasting, and general one-upmanship between friends and relations. Colleagues of ex-President Bush were particularly irked by the round-robin they received from George Sr. and Barbara this Christmas: "Young George W. is getting on just fine in his new job of President of the United States (thanks for the help, Jeb!). He is looking forward to starting World War III in the new year and Dad has been helping him find Iraq on the old family atlas. Coincidentally, this is also the time that he'll be beginning his campaign for reelection, and as Dubya says: 'I will not be impedimented!'"

Yes, believe it or not we are now more than halfway through the American electoral cycle, which is of course a far more important factor in the timing of any war than Iraqi winters or UN resolutions. You can understand why George W. Bush wants a military victory a year before his presidential election, but why do British troops need to be involved in his crude bid for electoral popularity?

Apart from all the death and suffering that British soldiers would inflict upon the already oppressed Iraqi people, the troops themselves would be at great risk of being killed, injured, or being entertained by Bob Hope. So wouldn't it be safer and far more honest if our boys were simply deployed in key marginal states across the pond to go canvassing for the U.S. Republican Party?

Instead of helping George W. Bush get reelected by joining a war in the Gulf, Her Majesty's armed forces would be parachuted into New Hampshire, where they could give out glossy leaflets saying "Re-elect Bush and Cheney 2004!" Dubya would still be grateful to Tony Blair, but no horrific war crimes would be committed and British servicemen would all come back safe and sound, except for the un-fortunate few who got lost in downtown Detroit.

Obviously, getting the British commandoes to do a little light political canvassing on a Saturday morning might involve a small amount of retraining. On their first attempt the elite forces would probably try to make contact with the voters by rappelling down from the roof and smashing through the upstairs windows, before detonat-ing stun grenades and smoke canisters. The residents, lying quiver-ing on the floor with a British army boot pressed down on their heads and an SA-80 assault rifle pointing at their temples, would then be asked a couple of politely worded questions about their current vot-ing intentions. And when they stammered that they would probably be voting for Ralph Nader, they'd be shot through the back 127 times. So the British army's usual approach is probably going to need ton-ing down a bit, though in its favour no one would accuse these par-ticular Republican canvassers of being soft on gun control.

Other British servicemen could be brought in as well. Instead of blowing up Baghdad, the RAF could just blow up thousands of red, white, and blue balloons. Chieftain tanks could be converted to fire tickertape and streamers, and the band of the Royal Marines could learn to trumpet their way through such U.S. election classics as "Simply the Best" and "You Ain't Seen Nothing Yet."

Of course we would all prefer it if the delivery of U.S. Republican Party leaflets could be done by the whole of the United Nations working together. But if the UN fails to take this historic opportunity to make itself relevant to the post 9/11 global scenario and it falls to U.S. and British forces to get George Bush reelected on our own, then we will not shirk from our moral duty to mobilise our troops to give out little lapel buttons with pictures of George W. to key voters in swing states.

Between you and me, there is another reason why this is by far the best solution. During the last Gulf war, there were so many military cock-ups and disasters that you can be sure that the same thing would happen if the U.S. and British armies were in charge of Bush's reelection campaign. The 1991 conflict saw allied troops killed by friendly fire, Patriot missiles repeatedly failing to knock out Scuds, and British troops being dropped in the wrong place with the wrong equipment. Bringing all this inexpertise to bear on Bush's election campaign is the only chance that the Democrats have.

So call up the reservists, send our boys over the Atlantic with their jamming rifles and their crashing Royal Navy destroyers, and, Godspeed, with our help the Global Village Idiot will be cast out of the White House in 2004.

Some have said that it is not the job of the British army to bring about "regime change" in a sovereign country. But in Bush's case I'm sure we can make an exception.

OFF THE WALL

8 February 2003

Why is everybody so quick to label Michael Jackson? Who among us can honestly say we haven't gone shopping and bought things we didn't really need? Who hasn't wished they could change their appearance a little? Who hasn't built their own private funfair, zoo, and fantasy park and got twelve-year-old kids to come over and stay the night in their bedroom? Okay, so just Michael then.

Martin Bashir's documentary was certainly compelling entertainment, especially since the Victorians stopped those tours through the lunatic asylums. We learnt that Michael wants his kids to have a happier childhood than he had. So he calls his son "Blanket." Yup, that sounds fine to me, I can't see any school bullies or sadistic teachers finding anything strange or laughable in that. In any case, when they're older, kids with unusual names always have the option of switching to their more conventional middle name, which in this case happens to be "Duvet." Michael Jackson's attempt to bottle-feed the baby did not fill one with confidence. There was an incredible amount of shaking going on, probably coming from the baby, who at that moment looked up to realise that this complete weirdo was his dad. But young Blanket is rapidly growing up to be a normal toddler and should be moonwalking any day now.

Another great moment was the sight of Michael going shopping. He dashed around a boutique crammed with ornate gold vases and giant jewel-encrusted urns, each costing tens of thousands of dollars, buying everything in sight while the store owner rubbed his hands like Uriah Heep behind him. I wish this scene had been filmed in Britain. "Ooh, no sorry, that's a display model I'm afraid and we won't have any more of those for another six to eight weeks." "But look, here's a million in cash—just let me have whatever you've got." "Nah, sorry, you have to order those in advance."

Of course the element that has grabbed all the media attention has been Jackson's relationship with a twelve-year-old boy. The parents of young Gavin are apparently perfectly happy for their son to go and sleep in Michael Jackson's bed. It's marvelous that such trust still survives in this world, that they can confidently send little Gavin off with his overnight bag, his toothbrush, and half a dozen hidden microphones while a crack team of private detectives and lawyers are parked in a mobile listening command center at the bottom of the lane praying that this will be the night they can hit Jacko with a billion-dollar lawsuit.

"Did you have a nice time at your friend's, dear?"

"Yes Mommy."

"Damn! You mean you didn't get trampled by one of his pet elephants or anything?"

I wonder if Michael ever goes back for a sleepover at Gavin's house.

"Hello Michael, we've put up the camp bed for you in Gavin's room, and got the oxygen tent down from the loft, and put up sun screens and hired a few aardvarks and camels to wander about the place to make you feel at home. Now would you like some ice cream, dear—it's five million dollars a scoop?"

Of course it is not normal or healthy for a forty-four-year-old man to have twelve-year-old boys over to stay, but what is it about our society that makes us so eager to scream "pedophile" before we're sure what is really going on? It seems more likely that Jacko, as part of his rather tragic childlike behaviour, is having "other" kids over to stay. Yet since the film was broadcast there has been an almost tangible hunger to brand Jackson as a pederast because in the modern Salem witch hunts it's been a few weeks since the last public show trial and the mob are screaming for more. We've had pediatricians attacked because people got that confused with pedophile. Who's next? I've got relations in Ireland called "Paddy O'Farrell"; that sounds a bit like "pedophile," maybe the mob should storm their houses as well. And as for Iraqi pedophiles posing as asylum seekers, well they're the worst of the lot.

The eagerness to tar Jacko with the worst possible brush is like one of the cheap thrills in his empty funfair. Yes, he is creepy and self-deluding but that doesn't automatically mean he must be evil. Nothing is black and white—especially in Michael Jackson's case. Apparently he was horrified by Bashir's documentary, saying, "I am surprised that a professional journalist would compromise his integrity by deceiving me." Blimey, he's even more detached from reality than we thought. Jacko's PR advisor should have warned him that doing this film was a bad idea, that it might be edited in such a way to make the singer seem a trifle eccentric. Sadly Michael's PR advisor is a llama and so was unable to do this. And so now Bashir has really put the star's nose out of joint. That should keep the plastic surgeons busy for a while.

THAT'S SLAUGHTERTAINMENT!

28 March 2003

The auditions to be Saddam Hussein's lookalike must be rather nervous affairs. All of Iraq's finest impressionists are summoned to the imperial palace, along with makeup artists, prosthetics experts, and the proprietor of "Moustaches 'R' Us." And then the Iraqi equivalents of Dana Carvey or Robin Williams have to stand before the brutal, vain, and famously short-tempered dictator and do their very best parody of him.

"Why are you twitching like that? I don't twitch!" barks Saddam as the Republican Guards try to suppress their laughter at the brilliance of the caricature. "We will defeat the American criminals . . ." continues the impressionist, twitching satirically as the soldiers collapse into uncontrollable laughter which they have to pretend are tears of love for their glorious leader. "And you are nowhere near handsome enough—why have you got a great big bulbous nose, I don't have a bulbous nose. We should get Richard Gere to be my lookalike."

With an atmosphere like this it's no wonder that Saddam's broadcasts end up being such dull and unwatchable affairs. The format is wooden and old-fashioned—with none of the intimacy or clever camera tricks that Western broadcasters have learnt. For example

Saddam would surely benefit from having a co-presenter, someone
with whom he could flirt on the Breakfast Time sofa before they
glanced through next week's newspaper headlines. "So Kelly, what
is next Wednesday's *Baghdad Times* saying . . ." he could ask with a
little wink. "Well Saddam, they've got you leading the victory parade over the vanquished Americans—and very handsome you look
too!" and they'd share an affectionate giggle as they cut to their resi-
dent zany weatherman predicting a light southeasterly breeze giving
way to huge clouds of oily smoke all over the country.

So apart from losing the military battle Saddam is also currently
losing the propaganda war. These days military spending is wasted if
you don't have the media backup to show the war from your view-
point. Alfred Hitchcock maintained that in a thriller the audience's
sympathies had more to do with where you placed the camera than
it did with accepted notions of morality. Take an everyday burglary,
for example. Film it from the victim's point of view, following him
as he walks nervously down the stairs because he's heard an intruder,
and you are obviously on the homeowner's side. But if the camera
had followed that burglar through the window and then suddenly he'd
heard someone coming down the stairs, you'd think "Oh no, quick,
get out!" And in this war, it's the intruders who have got the most
cameras. The Americans understand the Hitchcock Principle all too
well, which is why they built an enormous media center in the middle
of the desert almost before they did anything else.

More problematic Hollywood rules also apply, of course. The attention span of the modern audience is nowhere near as long as it
used to be. In centuries gone by not only were the plays and epic
poems much longer but the wars were too. But there's no way that a
modern scheduler could tolerate a six-year-long war today, not with
all the competition from the movie channels and reality TV shows.
That's why these days we go to war only against really easy opponents,

to make sure it's all over before we start reaching for the remote control. Otherwise they'd have to come up with new ways to keep us all interested—introducing *Pop Idol*–style phone votes to let the viewers decide who wins the mother of all battles. "If you want George Bush to win the war, phone or text the number on your screen now! If you want Saddam Hussein to win, phone this second number and hold for a visit from the CIA. . . ."

As it is, the new concept of twenty-four-hour slaughtertainment that's hit the airwaves is still compulsive television. The Oscars have had their lowest audience for years, because viewers want to catch the ending of the action adventure movie happening over on CNN. Perhaps this branch of show biz should have its own awards ceremony. Best supporting actor: Tony Blair. Best special effects: the U.S. Air Force. Best editing: award to be shared among all the American news channels. George Bush would go up to the podium to collect his special award: "I would like to thank my dad, without whom this war would not have been possible." And then there would be a little bit of controversy and the microphone would disappear into the lectern because one or two speakers used the occasion to criticize Hollywood films they'd seen that didn't quite work for them.

Except that they probably know it was Hollywood that taught them all the rules. America's point of view is dictated by the "p.o.v." in the movie director's meaning of the phrase. More westerners would have cried at the close-up human fiction in *Saving Private Ryan* than shed tears to see real-life explosions lighting up a distant Baghdad. No wonder the U.S. military was so keen to destroy Baghdad's main television station this week. Mao said that power grows out of the barrel of a gun. Now it comes out of the end of whichever gun has the cameras right behind it.

FREE MARKET FORCES

4 April 2003

*T*he following article is reprinted from the journal of the Washington Freedom Association, which has been hugely influential in shaping George Bush's foreign policy due to its uncompromising far-right Republican outlook in easy-to-read large print.

The war is now two weeks old and it seems incredible to many of us on Capitol Hill that Saddam Hussein has not yet surrendered. Has his translator not explained to him exactly what George Bush said, that "Baghdad will endure bombardmentalisation"? That "the Iraqi people must be freed from this tyrannosaurus regime"? What bit of "nonconditional capitulisation" does Saddam not understand?

The Washington Freedom Association is of the opinion that American foreign policy and the principles of free enterprise must go hand in hand. Yet we are permitting this war to be pursued by the federal government instead of outsourcing the operation to American private companies. War pursued by central government necessitates higher levels of federal taxation and is thus incompatible with the very freedom for which American service personnel are risking their lives. "Free enterprise warfare" would not only result in an army unfettered by federal bureaucracy, but by fielding an army employed by a limited company rather than a nation-state, troops would not be impeded by excessive petty international regulations such as the Geneva convention. In addition the boost to share prices of the companies conducting the conflict would have a regenerative effect on the U.S. economy as whole. Already a number of private companies have put in tenders to the State Department to take over the running of the Iraq war. Our finest supermarkets already have a large supplies of guns and ammunition on their shelves, Exxon has extensive experience in laying waste to large areas of countryside, Enron is looking for new spheres of influence, and there are many more companies that so enthusiastically share the president's vision of freedom that they contributed to his election campaign.

The idea is already a reality. To pilot the idea of "free market forces" a small squadron of privatized vehicle immobilizers from the Bronx was recently dispatched to secure strategic bases in Iraq. Admittedly early reports of this covert operation have been disappointing. Although a number of key bridges, power stations, et cetera were successfully neutralized, it seems that despite their extensive know-how the clampers destroyed major sections of infrastructure in the wrong country. Reports from Iran indicate that significant levels of hostility were provoked by these private contractors blowing up the wrong nation. However, the former traffic officers were then able to bring all their experience to bear, refusing to enter into any dialogue or even make eye contact with the so-called victims, and instead impassively filled out their paperwork before handing them a pro forma letter explaining how to appeal against an allegedly erroneous carpet bombing.

Teething problems are to be expected of course, but by outsourcing military operations the secretary of defence will be freed up to concentrate on the more appropriate diplomatic work of central government, extending full-spectrum dominance across the globe. It is not sufficient that the United Nations has been sidelined while there remain countless international organizations operating independently of American interests and security. It has come to our attention for example that every four years there takes place an event known as the Soccer World Cup, in which American teams have repeatedly been denied the freedom to field a team reflecting superior U.S. economic and military strength. Instead FIFA has unilaterally decided that the United States may field only eleven players, the same number permitted to third world countries such as Brazil and France. Like the UN, FIFA cannot be permitted to dictate the rules of engagement where American participants are involved and English president Toby Blare has promised he will back a rule change permitting a quarter of a million U.S. soccer players on the field at any one time. Similarly the organizers of the Miss World competition will no longer be permitted to allow winners from noncompliant nation-states. France will only be allowed to enter a man.

This will be a world in which opponents of liberty will be rendered inoperable. Enemies of free speech will be silenced. Iraq will be just the first country to benefit from the opportunity of reconstruction by U.S. companies after the bombing has been completed. Saddam knows that our democratic ideals will not permit us to see his son installed as Iraqi leader. George Bush is against this and so was George Bush Sr. when he was president. He cannot be permitted to cling to power without the democratic backing of his people. Saddam Hussein, that is, not George Bush.

Gary T. Bush is the nephew of the president and owns an emergent enterprise opportunity taking over the execution of prisoners in private penitentiaries in Texas and Florida.

MCDONALD'S TO GO, PLEASE

11 April 2003

This was truly an historic week as a much-hated regime finally seemed to lose its grip amid scenes of jubilation across the world. The McDonald's Information Minister, dressed in the official stripey uniform and proudly wearing his three stars that he received for managing to work in one of their restaurants for more than a month, appeared before the world's press angrily denying that the fast-food giant had finally lost the burger war. "Our heroic leader Ronald McDonald has scored another momentous victory," he declared as the famous Golden Arches came crashing to the ground behind him. "Our glorious Egg McMuffins have never been more popular!" he shouted as the share price tumbled and outlets were being closed around the world.

Meanwhile the whereabouts of Ronald McDonald himself remain a mystery. Some reports claim he may have died of heart failure after a lifetime of eating saturated burgers. Though the figurehead's iconic pictures are still displayed all across the crumbling McDonald's empire, many believe that it was a lookalike clown used in the recent propaganda film shown on Western television featuring him giving out balloons to young children. There is of course still much anxiety for the future. Huge reserves of oil can be found in their hamburgers and who knows what dangerous chemicals may yet be found when the inspectors go back into the restaurants. Ordinary McDonald's employees seemed dazed and confused in the midst of the crisis. Asked by a journalist if she could have evidence of the brutality of the regime, a pale and poorly fed looking young worker just stared blankly and asked, "You want fries with that?"

There is a rather satisfying symmetry that the most symbolic American corporate brand should be plunged into crisis just as the U.S. army is reasserting the military dominance of the world's only superpower. You might say that it was a delicious irony, but that adjective doesn't really feel appropriate here. The more aggressively that the old "military-industrial complex" asserts the rights of U.S. companies to trade around the world, the less the global consumer wants to hand it their cash. Hostility to the brand is such that earlier this week a bomb went off in a McDonald's in Beirut. It could have been really dangerous, but fortunately no one bought any Big Macs because as I say, a bomb went off. A few years ago there was an extended battle as the citizens of the poshest part of North London attempted to prevent a branch of McDonald's opening in their neighbourhood. The Hampstead residents wanted something more useful in their High Street, like an antique clock restorer's.

The brand that says "America" has lost its appeal. The world has taken a big bite of the American dream and is now feeling a bit queasy. In response to the first-ever loss in its fifty-five-year history, the American fast food giant has announced that it is going up-market. So soon you'll be able to see teenagers hanging around in bus shelters eating McChateaubriand and McCaviar with their bare hands. Obviously when the corporation says "up-market" they won't be going as far as indulging in unnecessary ostentatious extras such as cutlery. But in the future you will get a better class of worm in your filet o' fish.

Despite the attempt at rebranding the McDonald's share price has failed to recover. Maybe they should make the shares a bit more attractive by giving away little free gifts with them. Then embarrassed middle-class parents would say, "Well, we wouldn't normally buy a stake in the McDonald's Corporation but little Timmy had been desperate for the wind-up plastic dinosaur . . ."

McDonald's remains the most potent symbol of the freedoms for which the American troops have been fighting these past few weeks: the freedom of choice to have the same food served by the same corporation in every high street in the world. The only minor rules are that any employees attempting to form a union will be instantly sacked, any workers attempting to speak out against the corporation will be hit with massive lawsuits, and if you haven't got chronic acne, well, don't even think about applying for a job. Their fast-food mentality has spread to everything; U.S. foreign policy is quick and easy and don't think about the consequences: "Big Mac to go . . . fries to go . . . United Nations to go." And despite closing hundreds of outlets in the West, McDonald's are still seeking to expand in the third world and soon there will be very few cities in the world without a discarded vanilla shake splattered across the pavement. The West has got wise, so let's force the stuff down the throats of the rest of the world. So that's what this war was all about. Opening soon, McDonald's Restaurant, Al-Takhrir Square, Baghdad. Surely the Iraqis have suffered enough?

THE THIEF OF BAGHDAD

18 April 2003

The Baghdad branch of Neighbourhood Watch has been completely overwhelmed this week. "If you notice anyone behaving in a vaguely suspicious manner, please contact the police immediately," say their little signs on the lampposts, but these were all brazenly nicked along with everything else in the city that wasn't nailed down.

As the war stumbled to a confusing and chaotic end, lawlessness swept across the country as thousands of people helped themselves to computers, stereos, and other electrical goods. Such is the state of anarchy in the country that many of them haven't even sent off the little guarantee postcards yet. Western leaders have been reluctant to condemn the looters, perhaps because the clamor for material goods is partly what this war was all about: bringing Western style consumerism to a former Islamic "socialist" republic. With sufficiently aggressive advertising, within a few weeks the rioters will become vaguely dissatisfied with that Sony Playstation they seized and will feel the urge to go out and loot the new Playstation 2 with integral DVD player.

Meanwhile in Iraq's own version of *Supermarket Sweep*, the population have been fighting their way out of the stores with as much as they could carry (though there was a separate aisle for those looting eight items or less). Particularly popular were all the goods with special promotional stickers on them: "All this week—two for the price of none!" or "Steal one—get another one free!" And then isn't it always the way—you load up the car with looted goods, check the wads of banknotes you grabbed when they said "Do you want any cash back?," and then you realize you forgot to get your parking money back from the girl on the till.

In the traditional Arab markets traders attempted to haggle with the mob as they eyed the various trinkets and souvenirs on display.

"That is a beautiful hand-carved statue, sir. That is 100 dinar."

"Hmmm . . . tell you what—I'll give you zero dinar for it."

"All right, 80 dinar—I can't go lower than that, sir, look at the craftsmanship . . ."

"No, I think I'm going to stick with zero dinar actually . . ." said the looter as he brandished an old Russian machine gun.

"Um, well you drive a hard bargain. Zero dinar is my final price—take it or take it."

The former palaces of the Ba'ath leadership were also stripped, and the gold taps and erotic paintings are expected to fetch a fortune if anyone can transport them to a flea market. In wartime the media have a duty to convey a certain number of disturbing images, but showing us Saddam Hussein's taste in art is probably going too far. Snakes wrapping themselves around missiles being ridden by naked women; surely the artist will have to stand trial for crimes against humanity. I suppose he was just grateful for the work after he lost that job designing all those 1970s heavy metal album covers.

Some commentators attempted to argue that this was the dispossessed taking back what was rightfully theirs—but the looting of the palaces probably had more to do with the mob knowing where all the best stuff would be. Once they'd symbolically pulled down one statue, they forgot about the politics and got on with helping themselves to as much gear as possible. Which is why their former dictator managed to hide so easily; in the midst of all the chaos Saddam simply painted himself in metallic paint and is standing very very still in a busy town square somewhere.

Gradually, it seems, some sort of order is being restored in the cities, with some stolen goods even being returned (although the Baghdad branch of the Gap is now refusing to exchange looted clothes for a different size). But just when we thought the lawlessness was over, even more blatant incidents of looting have begun out of sight of the television cameras. With handkerchiefs masking half their faces, two rioters roughly the height of George Bush and Donald Rumsfeld kicked in the gates of Iraq's largest oilfield and started to grab all the keys of the oil tankers. International onlookers were powerless to prevent the illegal behaviour of these heavily armed looters and billions of dollars worth of crude oil, gas, and petroleum were seized, not to mention all the bumper stickers. "Yee-haw! It's all ours!" laughed the bandits, "millions of barrels of the stuff! We can just help ourselves and no one can stop us!" shrieked the gray-haired one as he filled up the first tanker and headed for home. "Yup, and this mask guarantees my anonymousinity!" said his leader. So after all these years there really is such a person as the Thief of Baghdad. Except strangely his accent sounded vaguely Texan.

AN AMERICAN IN PARIS (IN A SHERMAN TANK)

25 April 2003

This week another dangerous dictatorship has been added to the "Axis of Evil." Forget Syria, North Korea, and Iran; the next rogue state on the United States hit list appears to be France. Colin Powell declared on Wednesday that France will have to "face the consequences" of failing to back the United States on the UN Security Council, and all-out war can now only be a matter of time.

A few weeks back French fries were renamed "Freedom Fries"— which is clearly a far more sensible choice than our awkward English word "chips." Since then American makers of French polish and French horns have gone bankrupt and teenage boys have patriotically been attempting to persuade their girlfriends to try "freedom kissing." As Gallic food products are boycotted, exports of British cheeses to the United States are up with the finest Roquefort and Camemberts being replaced by British supermarkets' own brand of Microwavable Cheese Strings. If you are going to boycott a European economy, at least pick one with appalling food exports. "May I order the Châteauneuf du Pape?" "I'm afraid not, sir, but we can offer you this British gooseberry Riesling as an alternative."

Now an extensive UN dossier has been published, giving detailed accounts of French abuses of human rights. There are disturbing reports of nonchalant shrugging by French waiters. CNN has broadcast astonishing footage of French bureaucrats actually being rude and obstructive to foreigners, though surely this must have been faked. American mothers have been appalled by photographs of French women having a glass of wine when pregnant, though there is also a certain amount of pity for a population forced to watch all those intellectual French films that won the *oeuf d'or* at the Bruges film festival. But what's really annoyed the Americans is the provocative way they eat all this fancy rich food and just don't seem to get fat. The French must fall into line with Western levels of obesity or face the consequences. George Bush is now drawing up a list of the most wanted Frenchmen, which so far names only Gerard Depardieu and Babar the Elephant.

Hostility between the United States and France goes back quite a few years. A lot of bad feeling was created by the Louisiana Purchase when Napoleon's real estate agent managed to get the price up by claiming that there was another couple who were also very interested.

"They're bluffing . . ." said the American president, but Mrs. Jefferson had fallen in love with the big garden with that pretty two-thousand-mile river frontage onto the Mississippi. "I'm going to tell them that there's a few other properties that we're going to look at . . . I'll say we might decide to buy Florida off the Spanish instead. . . ."

"But darling, we could lose it altogether . . . and look at the realtor's details: 'A rare opportunity to purchase this 828,000-square-mile estate with its own mountain range, plains, lakes, and several outbuildings.' Oh darling, can we, please, please, please . . ." she begged, staring at the picture in *Country Life*. But of course when they moved in it was nothing like the description, half of it was swamps and deserts and the neighbours were unfriendly and kept threatening to scalp everyone. America sulked for a century and refused to forward all the mail. Then in 1966 President de Gaulle took France out of NATO and said all American troops should leave French soil. ("Does that include the dead ones?" quipped an American cynic at the time.) The United States then had to find another way to install American service personnel there, and this was the origin of Disneyland Paris. It was very hard to argue with Ronald Reagan at the best of times, but when he had this idea that thousands of U.S. marines should be stationed in northern France hidden inside Mickey Mouse and Goofy costumes, they thought he'd finally flipped. Battle-weary soldiers were kitted out in their new uniforms as Sneezy or Baloo the Bear. B-52 pilots were retrained to man Space Mountain and the flying Dumbo ride and amazingly the plan worked. The soldiers were delighted that the locals seemed to wave and cheer them every day as they rode past on the way to Sleeping Beauty's castle. Never before had U.S. troops been hugged and photographed with their arms round the native population.

But all this is now set to change when these agents suddenly reveal themselves at the outset of America's cunning plan to bring about regime change in Paris. The bombing of French cities begins next month, although no doubt those obstinate French politicians will find some reason to object to this as well. All the White House seeks is a French president who'll back the United States, a leader who'll support America whatever its policies. No wonder Tony Blair's been having those extra French lessons.

I DON'T WANT SPAM!

23 May 2003

Millions of men in Britain are getting private e-mail messages suggesting they might want to have their penises enlarged. "How did they know?" they are thinking. "Who told them? Was it Janice in accounts after last year's Christmas party? That's not fair, I was drunk and it was cold on that fire escape. . . ." Of course part of them suspects this is just another bit of "spam"—the unsolicited junk e-mail that is swamping the Net—but they're not going to shout about it just in case. Perpetrators of these scams must depend on this sort of embarrassment. If the operation went horribly wrong, you're not going to go on some TV consumer show and say, "Okay it used to be small but at least it worked. But now just look at what a botch job they made of it. . . ." And so unscrupulous businesses have continued to bombard our electronic in-boxes with offers of Viagra, free passwords to Internet porn sites, and special software designed to block unwanted e-mails.

Spam is the small ads section of the global village newspaper. And yesterday Yahoo! predicted that soon spam will overtake the number of normal e-mails flying around cyberspace. Just as the small ads of a local rag reveal what its readership is really thinking about (answer: sex and money), so the most common junk e-mail messages offer hard-core pornography and confidential money transfers out of Nigeria. It's hard to know which is more depressing: the baseness of human nature that this reveals or the stupidity of all the greedy people who fall for these scams. "Wow, what a fantastic offer! I transfer $200 to this overseas bank account and they pay off all my credit card debts! I can't see how this could possibly go wrong!" If I want to spend hundreds of pounds for absolutely nothing in return, I'll stick to holistic healing, thank you very much.

Of course the problem of unsolicited mail is nothing new. When the Penny Post started in 1840, masked highwaymen would hold up the mail coach and go through all the letters to see what goodies they might steal. "Ha-harrr! What do we have here? Hmm, offers to apply for a new type of credit card and forty-seven Sears catalogues. Damn!" And now in the twenty-first century, electronic mail involves so many hours sorting through all the junk that frankly you'd be better off popping that letter into a pillar box. Computer programs have been designed to randomly mix letters and numbers which are then combined with Internet service providers. For example, there's bound to be a *billgates1@hotmail.com*; in fact I think this was the very first e-mail account ever set up. And then Bill just sat at his computer for a few weeks feeling vaguely disappointed every time he checked his e-mails. Most of the invented e-mail addresses bounce back to the sender but millions more do exist and thus a message will suddenly pop up on your computer screen making you wonder where they got your address from. Either that or you entered it on that form that said "Yes, I would like to know more about online casinos and the world's smallest remote-control car."

It's estimated that spam currently costs businesses nine billion pounds a year, although I can never quite understand how they work these figures out. The presumption is that if people weren't wasting their time deleting e-mails, they'd be hard at work increasing company profits. In fact they'd only be wasting their time with some other mindless computer diversion, like playing Minesweeper or entering their own name on Google and then being slightly indignant that there were lots of other "David Smith"s around the world.

However, not content with being at war with drugs and terrorism, America has now declared war on spam as well. Last month the state of Virginia (home of America Online) outlawed the sending of unsolicited e-mails, making it a class 6 felony carrying a five-year prison term (or ten years for anyone who on hearing the word "spam" starts to recite the Monty Python sketch). The new law also gives the state the right to seize the assets of these companies, which is how the governor explained all those boxes of Viagra that his secretary found in the filing cabinet. There remains the slight problem that the Internet is no respecter of national borders or regional laws, but if those Russian gangsters did ever decide to move to Virginia and go public about their business practices they could be in serious trouble. Opponents claim that this law is in breach of America's sacred First Amendment: "Congress shall make no law abridging the freedom of speech, or of the press; or the right of the people to send out thousands of e-mails an hour offering live web-cams of group sex featuring pre-op transsexuals." But other U.S. states and EC governments look set to follow and then they will tell all the computer users of the world about their new legal rights and these new protections. And we'll see this historic message in our in-box and think, "Well that looks dodgy, I'm deleting that one for starters . . ."

UNITED ~~NATIONS~~ STATES

11 June 2003

Hans Blix had never planned to be a United Nations weapons inspector. But when he filled out one of those multiple-choice questionnaires at school, ticking off all his interests and qualifications, that's just what came out of the computer. His sister got "nurse," his brother got "engine driver," and Hans got "United Nations weapons inspector." That'll teach him to just tick all the boxes at random as a joke.

Hans Blix is stepping down from his controversial post at the UN but just before he packs away his souvenir Baghdad shaky snow scene, he has broken with the usual niceties of diplomatic language to attack the current U.S. administration. Claiming that he was smeared by "bastards" within the Pentagon, he added that there are hawks within the Bush regime who would like to see the United Nations "sink into the East River." "I believe that there were consistent efforts to undermine me," he told reporters, as Donald Rumsfeld stood behind him tapping his forehead and miming that Hans had gone completely gaga.

Hans's leaving card is already being passed around the Pentagon and one or two of the comments certainly reveal a slight hostility toward the retiring diplomat. "Sorry you are leaving the United

Nations, Hans. THAT'S IF YOU CAN FIND THE GODDAMN DOOR TO YOUR OFFICE!!" or "Hope you like your present, Hans, though I expect you'll get a bigger one from your buddy Saddam."

Since he first went out to Iraq with his *Observer's Book of Weapons of Mass Destruction,* Hans Blix found himself to be a target for both sides in the dispute. Republican hawks felt that Blix was not doing his job properly because he failed to exaggerate the threat posed by Saddam Hussein. If they'd had their way he would have gone into the Baghdad marketplace urging reporters to wear helmets and protective clothing before they approached the fruit and vegetable stall. "Look at this—a weapon of mass destruction cunningly disguised as a grapefruit. Plus anthrax cluster bombs in the shape of bananas. And look at these black currants; if thrown at someone with sufficient force these could ruin a perfectly good white shirt."

Meanwhile the Iraqi government said that Blix was "a homosexual who went to Washington every two weeks to receive his instructions." This is of course completely untrue. His office was in New York. Blix says that he used to laugh off all these various smears when he told his wife about them, but constant attacks can get to you eventually. "Darling, did you find the TV remote control?" "LISTEN, I HAVEN'T FOUND IT YET, ALL RIGHT!!" he snapped. "IT'S NOT UNDER THE SOFA CUSHIONS OR BEHIND THE TELLY. I THINK IT MAY HAVE BEEN DESTROYED OR BURIED IN THE DESERT SOMEWHERE."

With only a few weeks before he steps down, the United Nations has just set up a committee to organize Hans's leaving party and they are expected to publish a preliminary 500,000-word feasibility study in 2009. Bush is looking forward to Blix's retirement because he was planning to combine the event with a surprise leaving party for the rest of the UN staff as well.

"Leaving party? I didn't know we were leaving!"

"That's the surprise!" says George.

For 2003 is the year that the United Nations died. The most re-
vealing thing about Blix's interview is his assertion that the Bush
administration saw the UN as an alien power.

For years Pentagon officials have been lobbying hard at the UN.
It's the name they don't like: "United Nations—there's something
not quite right about it," they say.

"We're prepared to compromise . . ." they say. "You can keep the
first word."

"United?"

"Yeah, but that second bit sounds wrong—what other words are
there?"

"United Countries?"

"No . . ."

"United Places . . ."

"No, no, there must be another word for nation or country . . ."

"State?"

"Hmmm . . . *United States*, yes that has a ring to it. So we'll call it
the "United States" with its headquarters in the United States. . . .
Now this UN flag; we're prepared to compromise: you can keep some
of the blue, but it needs some red and white stripes in there as well."

Then George W. Bush tried to hijack the UN. Delegates thought
it was just a routine peacetime trip; they were settling back in their
seats for a snooze when suddenly a scary-looking American president
broke through the flimsy doors into the United Nations's cockpit,
grabbed the controls, and attempted to steer the UN into a catastrophe. Will anyone have the courage to overpower him, they wondered,
or should they nervously sit it out, hoping that they might somehow
survive?

Of course he tried to appear conciliatory and courteous. But Bush's
speech to the UN in September was like a head teacher pretending

to respect the newly formed school council. It's not that he was patronising to the UN, but at one point he stopped his monologue and shouted, "Canada! Are you chewing? Get up here and spit it out!" His message was that the only way to ensure that UN policy was implemented around the world was to change it to American policy. Some of the more subversive translators were having great fun. Bush said, "Will the United Nations serve the purpose of its founding or will it be irrelevant?" And into the headphones of one European minister came the translation, "Listen suckers, I'm going to bomb who the hell I like, so to hell with the lot of you!"

"The world now faces a test and the UN a defining moment . . ." continued Dubya as African leaders heard him apparently saying, "I've never heard of half your countries! Why are you wearing those funny costumes? I might bomb you next! I've got B-52s and Side-winders and everything, neeeeeoooow, boom! Bang! Ker-pow!"

Admittedly the United Nations is not the speediest means of deciding policy. At the beginning of the Afghan conflict a UN committee sat down to hammer out a resolution and this week they nearly agreed on whether it was "Taliban" with an "i" or "Taleban" with an "e." But changing the world takes time. It is a laborious and painstaking process. In North London an extended campaign by local residents recently managed to prevent a branch of Starbucks opening in their area. In my road another Starbucks has just opened and someone keeps smashing the windows. (It's amazing what you can get the local scouts to do for a pound.) Bombing Baghdad was the diplomatic equivalent of protestors who smash windows. It makes them feel tough and hard, it's quick and easy, but it doesn't actually make anything better for the people who really need help. It's instant expresso politics-to-go. Meaningful change is brought about by long-term strategies, patience, painstaking persuasion, and taking people with you. We have to ensure that the United Nations is the ultimate

authority; the UN has to agree on a meaningful line and then eventually we might find a way to rid the world of the new Starbucks on
my road.

The clash between Islam and Western capitalism may seem a little
tougher to sort out, but quick wars don't bring long-term peace. Bush's
American foreign policy is like American television. It has to keep
jumping from one thing to another because the president has the
remote control in his hand and his attention span is very limited.
That thrilling adventure "Take Out the Taliban!" held his interest
for a short while, but now the explosive opening action sequence is
over and it's got bogged down in the complex story of rebuilding a
war-torn country. Bush's finger is hovering over that button itching
to see if there's any more exciting stuff somewhere else.

"Don't you want to stick with this and see how Afghanistan turns
out?" says Colin Powell.

"Nah, it's got boring now."

"But we don't even know if they catch bin Laden . . ."

"Ooh wow, look what's on CNN! 'Bombers Over Baghdad'! Let's
see if this baddie Saddam gets it instead. . . ."

The war on Iraq will bring new problems to replace the old ones
but I doubt if it will make the world a safer place. Perhaps the only
way to make U.S. policy successful is to radically change the aims.
Then as the troops are brought home and the flags are waved the
White House could declare that they'd definitely achieved all the ob-
jectives in "Operation Kill All the Wrong People and Make the Problem Much Worse."

In the meantime there seems to be no place for the UN in Dubya's
new world order and henceforth the United Nations will be bypassed
or disregarded. To get a sense of the crisis you only have to look at
the last debate in that famous chamber, Motion 762/a—"Is the
United Nations being ignored?" Well what does the American rep-

resentative have to say about this? "Er, he's not here, Mr. Chair, he said he had some shopping to do." "Oh. All right, what about the British delegate?" "Er, well he's not here either, I think he's carrying the shopping. . . ." The last few remaining delegates never heard any of this anyway; they were trying to surpass their high scores on "Snake" on their mobile phones.

With the UN being ignored to death, Dubya's secret plan will have worked and the organisation will be formally wound up. Hundreds of unemployed translators will be cast onto the streets of New York saying "Excuse me, can you spare some change please? Excusez-moi, avez-vous de la monnaie? Scusi, possa avere dei soldi per favore?" And brash posters will be slapped all over the historic building that offered the world so much hope in 1945. "United Nations—Closing Down Sale! Everything must go! International law, global security, and U.S. accountability! We've gone crazy! Third world aid—slashed! Development programmes, going fast! Hurry, hurry, hurry! It's the biggest sell-out in history!"

ACKNOWLEDGMENTS

ost of these columns were originally printed in *The Guardian* newspaper, and so to all the staff there, from the editor down to the proofreaders, I would like to say a big thnak yuo. For jokes that may have crept in from our old TV scripts I would like to thank Mark Burton and Pete Sinclair, though I should stress that any old gags were recycled for environmental reasons only. For helping me make these pieces more suitable for American audiences (i.e., telling Microsoft Word to find "socialist" and replace it with "liberal") I would like to thank Alex Barocas and my U.S. editor, Brando Skyhorse. Oh, and for warning me against the dangers of making an acknowledgments list a thinly disguised attempt at name-dropping, I'd also like to thank Philip Roth, the Dalai Lama, Eminem, Nicole Kidman, and Nelson Mandela.

A NOTE ON THE TYPE

The font used in this book is called Lucia Sans BT. It was developed in Italy in the 1950s and swiftly became a modern classic. Capturing the tidy simplicity of the basic Roman alphabet, it adds a light serif, making it particularly easy on the eye while looking crisp and elegant on the page. The space between the letters, while appearing uniform, is in fact dependent on the adjacent characters, and although the original designers specified the exact gap for most letter combinations, they did not foresee certain character sequences that appear in English but not in Italian. Where this situation has arisen we have had to make aesthetic judgments of our own, endeavouring at all times to remain true to the spirit of the font's original design. All right, I know you couldn't give a toss about the font, but we had to pad the book out another couple of pages and we couldn't think of anything else to put in. I'm the bloke who does the typesetting and no one cares what I think. It doesn't matter what I write here, no one's going to read it. Well at last I'm going to come out with it. I'm gay. There, I've said it. Forty years I've kept that a secret. I'm gay, I'm gay, I'm gay. God, that feels better. I'm very fond of you, Marjorie, but our marriage is a sham. I'm having a secret affair with a picture restorer called Kenneth. I haven't really been going to evening macramé classes all these years. Kenneth and I are going to open a little shop in Brighton. I'm leaving and that's it; you'll have to find another bridge partner for Tuesdays. But poor Marjorie, she'd be devastated. It's not her fault it's taken me thirty years of marriage to come out of the closet. No, actually I just couldn't do that to her. Please don't print this, I'll write it out again. I know the printers are waiting but please, let me just do another draft; if Marjorie reads this she'd kill herself, please. . . .